Contents

Tall Tale Heroes

Life for American pioneers was hard, and their work was often tedious. For entertainment, they told funny stories called "tall tales." The stories had larger-than-life characters and were filled with exaggerations. Two famous tall tale characters are Paul Bunyan and Pecos Bill.

Imagine a giant lumberjack who could topple an acre of trees with one hand. That was Paul Bunyan. Bunyan was so big that he had to eat 40 bowls of porridge just to whet his appetite. His faithful companion was an immense blue ox named Babe. Their rain-filled footprints became the 10,000 lakes of Minnesota. According to stories, surviving in the North Woods was also an achievement. One winter, it was so cold that Babe's milk turned straight to ice cream!

Do you know of any cowboy who would ride a horse named Widow Maker? That was Pecos Bill, who also galloped around on a mountain lion. Legend says that Bill fell from his parents' wagon when he was a baby. Coyotes rescued Bill and raised him in the wild. He could rope a whole herd of cattle at once, or even lasso a cyclone. And when he anticipated trouble, he carried a live rattlesnake as a whip. Bill's girlfriend was also famous for her frequent stunts. Slue-Foot Sue once took a pleasant ride on a giant catfish down the Rio Grande!

Find It! Read the spelling words.
Check off the words you can find in the story.

- [ ] tedious
- [ ] straight
- [ ] eagerly
- [ ] famous
- [ ] pleasant
- [ ] frequent
- [ ] acre
- [ ] anticipate
- [ ] achievement
- [ ] persuade
- [ ] campaign
- [ ] freighter

How many spelling words did you find? ______

Skills:

Spelling Words with Short and Long **a**, and Short and Long **e**

Spelling Theme Vocabulary

Visual Memory

Spelling Practice

Read and Spell	Copy and Spell	Spell It Again!
1. tedious	__________	__________
2. straight	__________	__________
3. eagerly	__________	__________
4. famous	__________	__________
5. pleasant	__________	__________
6. frequent	__________	__________
7. acre	__________	__________
8. anticipate	__________	__________
9. achievement	__________	__________
10. persuade	__________	__________
11. campaign	__________	__________
12. freighter	__________	__________

Searching for Words

Skills:

Visual Sequencing

Recognizing Spelling Words

Fill in the missing letters to make spelling words.

camp ____ ____ gn	____ ____ re	t ____ d ____ ous
fam ____ ____ s	antici ____ ____ te	pers ____ ____ de
fr ____ ____ ghter	ach ____ ____ vement	____ ____ gerly
fre ____ ____ ent	pl ____ ____ sant	str ____ ____ ght

Now, find and circle the spelling words in the word search.
Words can go across, down, or diagonally.

W R A T S E R B E E I L S
A T E D I O U S M U O P P
C S A P E R S U A D E S L
H I G O U N D S N T A T E
I F E T L A U Y A E Y R A
E R R E X O H P S U E A S
V T L E M S I V A O G I A
E A Y A Q C A M P A I G N
M N F O I U M C L E A H T
E G X T N P E D R I L T E
N E N I G A T N S E V B W
T A F R E I G H T E R S I

Skills:

Using Context Clues to Find Missing Words

Missing Words

pleasant	frequent	acre	freighter
persuade	achievement	famous	eagerly
campaign	tedious	straight	anticipate

Fill in the blanks with words from the spelling words above.

1. Paul Bunyan could topple an ______________________ of trees with one hand!
2. Pecos Bill could ______________________ trouble wherever he traveled.
3. Babe was as ______________________ as Paul Bunyan.
4. Life for American pioneers could be hard and ______________________.
5. One very cold winter, Babe's milk turned ______________________ to ice cream!
6. Surviving life in the harsh North Woods was quite an ______________________.
7. Slue-Foot Sue ______________________ awaited for Pecos Bill to return.
8. Pecos Bill went on a long ______________________ to rope herds of cattle.
9. Slue-Foot Sue took a ______________________ ride on a giant catfish.
10. I bet Babe could pull a ______________________ across all the lakes in Minnesota.
11. Paul Bunyan was a ______________________ visitor to the North Woods.
12. It wasn't easy to ______________________ Slue-Foot Sue to marry Pecos Bill.

Sentence Endings

Skills:

Using Correct Ending Punctuation

Identifying Different Kinds of Sentences

There are four kinds of sentences. Each kind requires specific ending punctuation.

- A declarative sentence is a statement. It ends with a period. (.)
- An interrogative sentence asks a question. It ends with a question mark. (?)
- An imperative sentence commands someone to do something. It ends with a period. (.)
- An exclamatory sentence shows strong feeling. It ends with an exclamation mark. (!)

Add the correct ending punctuation to each sentence. Identify each sentence by writing **declarative**, **interrogative**, **imperative**, or **exclamatory** on the line.

1. Pecos Bill rode a horse named Widow Maker ____ ____________
2. Wow, he could rope a whole herd of cattle at once ____ ____________
3. Could Paul Bunyan eat 40 whole bowls of porridge ____ ____________
4. Watch out, that porridge is hot ____ ____________
5. Read me a story about Slue-Foot Sue ____ ____________
6. She rode a giant catfish down the Rio Grande ____ ____________
7. How could anyone ride a catfish ____ ____________
8. I guess it must be a tall tale after all ____ ____________
9. Did Babe's milk really turn straight to ice cream ____ ____________
10. Hearing tall tales must have been pleasant ____ ____________
11. How did they make the 10,000 lakes of Minnesota ____ ____________
12. Help me write a tall tale for class ____ ____________

Skills:

Matching Words with Their Meanings

Vocabulary Match

Write the letter of the definition that matches each spelling word.

________	1. tedious	a.	an outstanding act or accomplishment
________	2. pleasant	b	with great anticipation
________	3. freighter	c.	directly
________	4. straight	d.	to look forward to; to expect
________	5. famous	e.	a series of actions in order to achieve something
________	6. achievement	f.	to convince
________	7. anticipate	g.	happening often
________	8. campaign	h.	enjoyable or giving pleasure
________	9. acre	i.	tiring and boring
________	10. eagerly	j.	widely known
________	11. persuade	k.	a ship that carries cargo
________	12. frequent	l.	a unit for measuring land

Spellamadoodle

Skills:

Writing
Spelling
Words

Write each spelling word on the outline of the drawing. You may use the words more than once. For fun, decorate the drawing.

pleasant	frequent	acre	freighter
persuade	achievement	famous	eagerly
campaign	tedious	straight	anticipate

Skills:

Writing a Description

My Tall Tale Hero

Paul Bunyan, Babe, Pecos Bill, and Slue-Foot Sue are tall tale heroes. Tall tales exaggerate a hero's strength, speed, adventures, and more. Think up some qualities for a tall tale hero. Will your hero be male or female? person or animal? What kinds of qualities will he or she have—strength? intelligence? Think of a good name for your hero and list his or her qualities below.

My tall tale hero's name is:

____

My tall tale hero looks like:

____

____

____

My tall tale hero can do these amazing things:

____

____

____

____

____

My tall tale hero is special because:

____

____

____

____

My Tall Tale

Now that you've invented your own tall tale hero, write a tall tale for him or her! Think of a fantastic adventure for your tall tale hero. Give specific details, and remember to exaggerate. Use some of the spelling words in your tale.

tedious	straight	eagerly	famous
pleasant	frequent	acre	anticipate
achievement	persuade	campaign	freighter

Skills:

Writing a Tall Tale

Using Spelling Words in an Original Composition

Edit Your Work

- ○ I used complete sentences.
- ○ I used correct spelling.
- ○ I used correct capitalization and punctuation.

Tall Tale Heroes

Find the correct answer. Fill in the circle.

1. Which of the following is an interrogative sentence?
   - ❍ Legends and tall tales are similar kinds of stories.
   - ❍ Have you ever written a tall tale?
   - ❍ Babe's milk got so cold it turned to ice cream!

2. Which of the following is an imperative sentence?
   - ❍ Coyotes raised Pecos Bill in the wild.
   - ❍ Pecos Bill carried a rattlesnake as a whip!
   - ❍ Read me a story about Paul Bunyan and Babe.

3. Which of these is a definition for the word *tedious*?
   - ❍ enjoyable
   - ❍ tired and boring
   - ❍ widely known

4. Which word is spelled correctly?
   - ❍ achievement
   - ❍ achevement
   - ❍ acheivement

Spelling Test

Ask someone to test you on the spelling words.

1. ____________________
2. ____________________
3. ____________________
4. ____________________
5. ____________________
6. ____________________
7. ____________________
8. ____________________
9. ____________________
10. ____________________
11. ____________________
12. ____________________

5. Write the sentence correctly.

the faimus hero eegerley cut down an acer of trees—an amazing acheivment

____

____

At Your Fingertips

Twins often have the same hair and eye color. But they don't have the same fingerprints or thumbprints. No two people have prints that are exactly alike. Fingerprints have distinct ridges, spirals, loops, splits, and dots. Although prints expand as a person grows, they don't change. Only deep injuries or disease can sometimes alter them.

In 1686, Professor Marcello Malpighi was the first to fully describe ridges, spirals, and loops in fingerprints. His descriptions are still used today. Sir Francis Galton, a British scientist, noted that fingerprints could be valuable to identify people. He said that the odds of two sets of fingerprints being the same were one in 64 billion! In 1892, he published a book entitled *Fingerprints.* It included the first scientific classification system. That year, a police officer in Argentina captured a fugitive who was wanted for murder. He was able to utilize a bloody fingerprint to prove her guilt. Fingerprints had become an important tool for the police and the courts.

In 1924, the United States Congress created the Identification Division of the F.B.I. Its files hold more than 40 million fingerprint records!

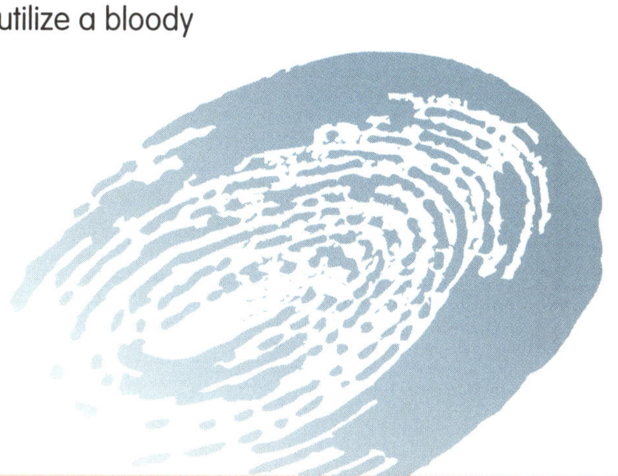

Find It! Read the spelling words.
Check off the words you can find in the story.

☐ although	☐ envelope	☐ often	☐ officer
☐ describe	☐ scientific	☐ distinct	☐ utilize
☐ valuable	☐ thumbprint	☐ fugitive	☐ customary

How many spelling words did you find? _____

Skills:

Spellings for Long and Short **o**, **i**, and **u**

Spelling Theme Vocabulary

Visual Memory

Spelling Practice

Read and Spell	Copy and Spell	Spell It Again!
1. although		
2. envelope		
3. often		
4. officer		
5. describe		
6. scientific		
7. distinct		
8. utilize		
9. valuable		
10. thumbprint		
11. fugitive		
12. customary		

Correct Spellings

Circle the words that are spelled correctly.

1.	valubel	valuable	valeble
2.	sientific	scuntific	scientific
3.	ulthogh	although	althoge
4.	envelope	envuloppe	anvelope
5.	thumprint	thumpprent	thumbprint
6.	fugitive	fugetiv	feugetive
7.	distente	distinct	distect
8.	utilize	uteliz	utulise
9.	dusrib	describe	discribe
10.	ofen	offten	often
11.	custumarry	costumery	customary
12.	officer	oficcer	offiser

Circle the misspelled words in the sentences. Write them correctly on the lines.

1. Using fingerprints is now custumarry for police offisers.

   ______________________ ______________________

2. You can even utelize fingerprints on envuloppes.

   ______________________ ______________________

3. A thummprint can be vallublе in solving a crime.

   ______________________ ______________________

4. How offen is a disteect fingerprint found?

   ______________________ ______________________

Skills:

Spellings for Long and Short **o, i,** and **u**

Spelling Theme Vocabulary

Visual Memory

Skills:

Matching Words with Their Synonyms and Antonyms

Synonyms & Antonyms

Draw a line between the two words that are synonyms (mean the same).

customary	explain
describe	runaway
distinct	usual
fugitive	useful
utilize	unique
valuable	use

Draw a line between the two words that are antonyms (mean the opposite).

customary	unimportant
distinct	rare
utilize	same
valuable	discard

Joining Sentences

A compound sentence is made by putting together two or more simple sentences containing related information.

- The parts are usually joined by a conjunction such as and, or, or but.
- A comma is placed before the conjunction.

I wrote a paper on fingerprints. I presented it to my class.

I wrote a paper on fingerprints, and I presented it to my class.

Skills:

Writing Compound Sentences

Using Commas and Conjunctions

Use conjunctions and commas to combine each pair of simple sentences into a compound sentence. Underline the conjunction.

1. I'm interested in police work. I don't want to be a police officer.

____

____

2. Fingerprints expand as a person grows. They don't change.

____

____

3. I love to study fingerprints. I would like to learn more about them.

____

____

4. I can be a police officer. I can be a firefighter.

____

____

5. Fingerprints are important. They have become a good tool for the courts.

____

____

6. DNA is also valuable. It has only recently been perfected.

____

____

Skills:

Visual Sequencing

Recognizing Spelling Words

Word Search

Find and circle the spelling words. Words can go across, down, or diagonally.

although	envelope	often	officer
describe	scientific	distinct	utilize
valuable	thumbprint	fugitive	customary

C	F	G	V	A	L	U	A	B	L	E	E	D	F
A	U	C	D	E	N	V	E	L	O	P	E	E	N
O	G	S	E	L	A	L	U	N	X	D	B	S	C
S	I	Z	T	C	N	I	T	S	I	D	Z	C	U
H	T	B	J	O	L	T	M	C	G	H	Y	R	F
X	I	T	H	U	M	B	P	R	I	N	T	I	F
A	V	H	W	X	U	A	T	U	N	L	W	B	O
N	E	O	F	J	N	M	R	X	G	E	D	E	O
L	I	U	T	E	C	E	R	Y	Z	U	J	V	F
C	V	L	T	H	B	U	P	I	T	P	N	G	F
T	E	F	F	O	D	E	L	S	C	Y	V	K	I
I	O	K	D	S	C	I	E	N	T	I	F	I	C
F	Z	B	U	W	T	W	N	T	M	G	F	B	E
E	T	H	G	U	O	H	T	L	A	Z	D	Y	R

Spellamadoodle

Skills:

Writing Spelling Words

Write each spelling word on the outline of the drawing. You may use the words more than once. For fun, decorate the drawing.

although	envelope	often	officer
describe	scientific	distinct	utilize
valuable	thumbprint	fugitive	customary

Skills:

Writing a Description

My Fingerprints

Use an ink pad to stamp your fingerprints in the boxes below. Be sure not to smudge them! Use a magnifying glass to examine your prints more closely. Knowing that fingerprints have distinct ridges, spirals, loops, splits, and dots, describe your prints. Be specific!

Right Hand				
Thumb	Index Finger	Middle Finger	Ring Finger	Pinky Finger
Left Hand				
Thumb	Index Finger	Middle Finger	Ring Finger	Pinky Finger

Right Hand

____

____

____

____

Left Hand

____

____

____

____

Mysterious Fingerprints

Skills:

Writing a Mystery Story

Using Spelling Words in an Original Composition

Detectives and police officers use fingerprints to solve crimes. Write your own mystery story in which fingerprints play an important role. How do the detectives finally solve the crime? Use as many spelling words as you can. If you don't have enough room, continue your story on another sheet of paper.

although	envelope	often	officer
describe	scientific	distinct	utilize
valuable	thumbprint	fugitive	customary

Edit Your Work

- ◯ I used complete sentences.
- ◯ I used correct spelling.
- ◯ I used correct capitalization and punctuation.

At Your Fingertips

Find the correct answer. Fill in the circle.

1. Which sentence has a conjunction in it?
   - ○ Some people's prints are similar.
   - ○ Some people's prints are similar, but no two are exactly the same.
   - ○ No two people's prints are similar.

2. Which sentence is a compound sentence?
   - ○ I could study fingerprints.
   - ○ I could study DNA evidence.
   - ○ I could study fingerprints, or I could study fingerprint evidence.

3. Which word is a synonym for *customary*?
   - ○ usual
   - ○ unusual
   - ○ useful

4. Which word is spelled correctly?
   - ○ utilise
   - ○ utilize
   - ○ utileze

Spelling Test

Ask someone to test you on the spelling words.

1. ____________________
2. ____________________
3. ____________________
4. ____________________
5. ____________________
6. ____________________
7. ____________________
8. ____________________
9. ____________________
10. ____________________
11. ____________________
12. ____________________

5. Write the sentence correctly.

   ulthogh detective walters found a thummprint on the envuloppe,
   he was unable to utulize it

   ____

   ____

Elizabeth Blackwell

There was a time when you wouldn't see a woman doctor anywhere. That was before Elizabeth Blackwell received her degree from Geneva Medical College on January 23, 1849. On that special occasion, she became the first woman doctor in the United States.

Elizabeth Blackwell was born in England in 1821. Her family soon moved to America. Her goal in life was to heal people. Everybody told her that the old-fashioned medical schools wouldn't accept a woman. Meanwhile, Blackwell studied medical books. She applied to the best medical schools. Finally, the male students of Geneva Medical College voted on her request. They voted to give her the opportunity to attend. Many thought Blackwell would fail. She did just the opposite. She was an outstanding student. Two years later, Elizabeth Blackwell graduated at the head of her class.

At first, no paying patients would come to her. Dr. Blackwell treated poor families for free, and they would recommend her to others. She created a hospital for women and children. She also founded a medical college for women. By 1910, when Dr. Blackwell died, more than 7,000 women were practicing medicine in the United States. Her quest for knowledge paved the way for the millions of women doctors who have followed in her footsteps.

Find It! Read the spelling words.
Check off the words you can find in the story.

- [ ] anywhere
- [ ] occasion
- [ ] everybody
- [ ] old-fashioned
- [ ] meanwhile
- [ ] footsteps
- [ ] opportunity
- [ ] outstanding
- [ ] recommend
- [ ] studied
- [ ] opposite
- [ ] knowledge

How many spelling words did you find? ______

Skills:

Compound Words

Spelling Theme Vocabulary

Visual Memory

Spelling Practice

Read and Spell	Copy and Spell	Spell It Again!
1. anywhere	__________	__________
2. occasion	__________	__________
3. everybody	__________	__________
4. old-fashioned	__________	__________
5. meanwhile	__________	__________
6. footsteps	__________	__________
7. opportunity	__________	__________
8. outstanding	__________	__________
9. recommend	__________	__________
10. studied	__________	__________
11. opposite	__________	__________
12. knowledge	__________	__________

Crossword Challenge

Complete the crossword puzzle using words from the spelling list.

anywhere	occasion	everybody	old-fashioned
meanwhile	footsteps	opportunity	outstanding
recommend	studied	opposite	knowledge

Across

3. to suggest as being good or worthy
5. a time when something happens
8. extremely good
9. no longer fashionable or popular
10. completely different
11. each and every person

Down

1. to have spent time learning a subject or skills
2. the things that someone knows; information
4. follow in someone's ________ (try to be like)
6. in or during the time between
7. in or to any place
8. a chance to do something

Skills:

Compound Words

Spelling Theme Vocabulary

Visual Memory

Word Meaning

Skills:

Making Compound Words

Spelling Theme Vocabulary

Visual Memory

Spell Check

Draw lines to make compound spelling words.

any	while
old-	standing
out	where
every	steps
mean	body
foot	fashioned

Circle the word in each row that is spelled correctly.

1.	oppertunite	opportunity	oporttunity
2.	reccomend	recommind	recommend
3.	meenwile	meanwhile	meanwille
4.	knowledge	knolege	knowlije
5.	footstepps	feetsteps	footsteps
6.	studyed	studdied	studied
7.	opposite	opossite	oposit
8.	everybody	evrybudy	everybodie
9.	oporttunity	opportunity	oppurtunite
10.	old-fashund	oldfashonned	old-fashioned
11.	enywhere	anywere	anywhere
12.	outstanding	outtstandin	outstandding

Pronoun Puzzler

Subject pronouns replace a noun used as the subject of a sentence.

I they you he she it we

Object pronouns replace a noun used after an action verb or a preposition.

me us him them you her it

Reflexive pronouns refer back to the subject.

myself yourself himself herself itself ourselves yourselves themselves

Skills:

Identifying and Using Subject, Object, and Reflexive Pronouns

Circle the correct pronoun or pronouns to complete each sentence. Then go back and write S for **subject**, O for **object**, or R for **reflexive** over the pronouns you circled. The first one has been done for you.

1. **You and me**/**You and I** should apply to medical school this fall. (S)
2. **Ourselves**/**We** are hoping to attend a university back East.
3. I gave **herself**/**myself** plenty of time to study for the test.
4. **Him and me**/**He and I** went to the library after school.
5. Terrance found **us**/**we** at a table behind the medical books.
6. The students **themselves**/**they** planned the event.
7. Elizabeth Blackwell enrolled **she**/**herself** at Geneva Medical College.
8. The male students at Geneva helped **herself**/**her** to get accepted.
9. **They**/**Themselves** voted on her request for admission.
10. Mrs. Ramirez gave **Josh and me**/**I and Josh** a special assignment.
11. **Us**/**We** will write a report about the life of Elizabeth Blackwell.
12. **She**/**Her** was the first woman doctor in America.

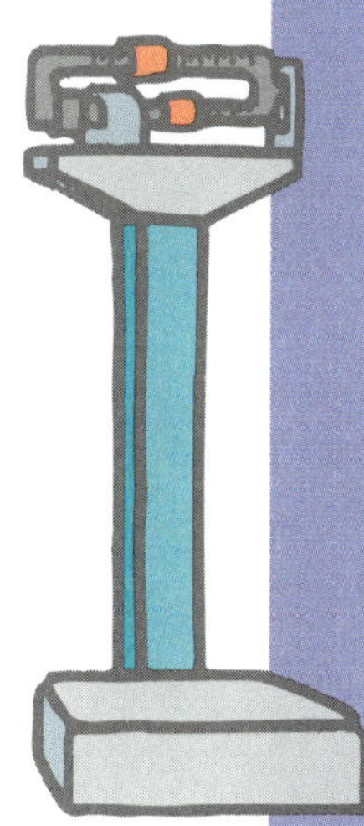

Skills:

Using Context Clues to Identify Missing Words

Writing Spelling Words

Missing Words

Complete the paragraphs using the spelling words.

anywhere	occasion	everybody	old-fashioned
meanwhile	footsteps	opportunity	outstanding
recommend	studied	opposite	knowledge

When Elizabeth Blackwell became a doctor, it was a very special ____________________. She had ____________________ medical books years before graduating from Geneva Medical College. She worked hard to gain the ____________________ she needed to be the first woman doctor in the United States.

It was a long road. ____________________ told her she wouldn't get accepted to medical school. Most medical schools were ____________________ and didn't admit women. ____________________, Elizabeth continued to study medical books. Instead of giving in, Elizabeth did just the ____________________. Twenty-nine schools denied her admission. The faculty of the Geneva Medical School was the only group to ____________________ her for admission. It was a great ____________________ for her. She became an ____________________ doctor and role model for women everywhere!

Many women have followed in Elizabeth Blackwell's ____________________ to become doctors themselves. Now, women doctors may be found ____________________ you look. Elizabeth Blackwell paved the way!

Spellamadoodle

Skills:

Writing Spelling Words

Write each spelling word on the outline of the drawing. You may use the words more than once. For fun, decorate the drawing.

anywhere	occasion	everybody	old-fashioned
meanwhile	footsteps	opportunity	outstanding
recommend	studied	opposite	knowledge

Skills:

Using Spelling Words in an Acrostic Poem

Poetry Time

Create an acrostic poem. Write a word or phrase that starts with each letter in the topic word. Use a dictionary and words in the story to help you.

B ________________________________

L ________________________________

A ________________________________

C ________________________________

K ________________________________

W ________________________________

E ________________________________

L ________________________________

L ________________________________

Special Firsts

Skills:

Writing a Personal Narrative

Elizabeth Blackwell became the first American woman doctor in January 1849. Think of important "firsts" in your own life. Have you ever won first place in a contest or competition? Do you remember the first time you saw snow or the ocean? Write about this special "first" below. Provide lots of descriptive details.

℞

✓ Edit Your Work

- ◯ I used complete sentences.
- ◯ I used correct spelling.
- ◯ I used correct capitalization and punctuation.

Elizabeth Blackwell

Find the correct answer. Fill in the circle.

1. Which sentence uses the pronoun correctly?
   - ❍ Can Dad help I study for this test?
   - ❍ Can Dad help myself study for this test?
   - ❍ Can Dad help me study for this test?
2. Which sentence uses the pronoun correctly?
   - ❍ The Millers gave himself a week to move in.
   - ❍ The Millers gave themselves a week to move in.
   - ❍ The Millers gave they a week to move in.
3. Which word is not a synonym for the word *outstanding*?
   - ❍ commonplace
   - ❍ exceptional
   - ❍ remarkable
4. Which word is spelled correctly?
   - ❍ recomend
   - ❍ recommend
   - ❍ reccommend

Spelling Test

Ask someone to test you on the spelling words.

1. ____________________
2. ____________________
3. ____________________
4. ____________________
5. ____________________
6. ____________________
7. ____________________
8. ____________________
9. ____________________
10. ____________________
11. ____________________
12. ____________________

5. Write the sentence correctly.

your knowllegde of this old-fashunned occasson is outtstunding

____

____

The Duckbilled Platypus

When people in England saw a duckbilled platypus for the first time, they didn't believe it was natural. They thought it was a joke. No furry creature had a bill like a duck and a tail like a beaver! The platypus is an egg-laying mammal called a "monotreme." The babies, known as "puggles," hatch from eggs. About the size of a small house cat, the amazing platypus lives in burrows near freshwater ponds and streams in Australia.

The duckbilled platypus is an efficient swimmer. Its oily outer hair is coarse and waterproof, while its undercoat is woolly and warm. *Platypus* means "flat-footed," and its flat webbed front feet work like paddles. The tail is perfect for steering and stores enough fat to help the platypus get through the winter. Its flexible bill is extremely sensitive to the touch. The platypus closes its eyes underwater and uses its bill to feel along in the mud, searching for tiny worms and snails.

The platypus may be cute, but beware! Males have a special feature of venomous spurs on their back legs. They can puncture a predator and inject a strong dose of venom. An adult human will probably survive the dose, but the wound is no pleasure. It causes extreme physical pain. So, it's best to leave the platypus alone.

Find It!

Read the spelling words.
Check off the words you can find in the story.

- [ ] creature
- [ ] feature
- [ ] puncture
- [ ] leisure
- [ ] pleasure
- [ ] natural
- [ ] enough
- [ ] physical
- [ ] efficient
- [ ] flexible
- [ ] oily
- [ ] turmoil

How many spelling words did you find? _____

Skills:

Patterns of **–ture** and **–sure**

Spelling Theme Vocabulary

Visual Memory

Spelling Practice

Read and Spell	Copy and Spell	Spell It Again!
1. creature	____________	____________
2. feature	____________	____________
3. puncture	____________	____________
4. leisure	____________	____________
5. pleasure	____________	____________
6. natural	____________	____________
7. enough	____________	____________
8. physical	____________	____________
9. efficient	____________	____________
10. flexible	____________	____________
11. oily	____________	____________
12. turmoil	____________	____________

Making Spelling Words

Fill in the blanks to make spelling words.

crea ____ ____ re	plea ____ ____ re	enou ____ ____
punc ____ ____ re	lei ____ ____ re	turm ____ ____ l
flex ____ ____ le	nat ____ ____ al	____ ____ ysical
effi ____ ____ ent	____ ____ ly	fea ____ ____ re

Choose and circle the correct spelling.

1. The male platypus's back legs **feechure**/**feature** venomous spurs.
2. This animal has **oily**/**oully**, coarse hair that is waterproof.
3. The male uses its spurs to **puncture**/**puntcher** and inject venom.
4. The duckbilled platypus is a strange-looking **creatcher**/**creature**.
5. Its webbed front feet work like **efficionte**/**efficient** paddles.
6. The venom from a platypus can cause intense **physical**/**fisical** pain.
7. This amazing animal hardly looks **natcheral**/**natural**!
8. A platypus is about big **enough**/**enuff** to be a house cat.
9. It is a **plessure**/**pleasure** to watch the babies, called puggles.
10. The platypus lives a life of **liessur**/**leisure** near freshwater ponds.

Skills:

Patterns of **–ture** and **–sure**

Spelling Theme Vocabulary

Visual Memory

Spelling Words in Context

Skills:

Patterns of **–ture** and **–sure**

Spelling Theme Vocabulary

Word Meaning

Writing Complete Sentences

What Does It Mean?

Draw a line to match each word with its meaning.

creature	an important part or quality of something
feature	normal or usual
puncture	a living being, human or animal
leisure	working very well; getting the job done
pleasure	free time; when you do not have to work
natural	as much as needed
enough	to make a hole in something
physical	covered with a thick, greasy liquid
efficient	a feeling of enjoyment or satisfaction
flexible	having to do with the body
oily	great confusion
turmoil	able to bend

Write a sentence using the spelling words *natural* and *creature*.

____

____

Write a sentence using the spelling words *leisure* and *pleasure*.

____

____

All in Agreement

Skills:

Writing Complete Sentences

Identifying and Using Subject/Verb Agreement

The verb in a sentence must agree in number with the subject.

- If the subject is singular, the verb must be singular.

  The puggle loves to snuggle.

- If the subject is plural, the verb must be plural.

  Capybaras love to swim.

If the subject/verb agreement is correct, write correct on the line. If the sentence/verb agreement is incorrect, rewrite the sentence correctly.

1. The platypus like to eat tiny worms and snails.

   ____

   ____

2. What else do you thinks it likes to eat?

   ____

   ____

3. Are platypuses more like mammals or birds?

   ____

   ____

4. Another monotreme are the spiny anteater.

   ____

   ____

5. Spiny anteaters lives in Australia and New Guinea.

   ____

   ____

6. This anteater eats ants and termites with its long sticky tongue.

   ____

   ____

Skills:

Visual Discrimination

Using Spelling Words

Secret Code

Write the letter that stands for each number to discover six of the spelling words.

a	b	c	e	f	g	h	i	l	m	n	o	p	r	s	t	u	x	y
1	2	3	4	5	6	7	8	9	10	11	12	13	14	15	16	17	18	19

1. ___ ___ ___ ___ ___ ___ ___ ___
13 7 19 15 8 3 1 9

2. ___ ___ ___ ___ ___ ___ ___ ___
5 9 4 18 8 2 9 4

3. ___ ___ ___ ___ ___ ___ ___ ___ ___
4 5 5 8 3 8 4 11 16

4. ___ ___ ___ ___ ___ ___ ___
5 4 1 16 17 14 4

5. ___ ___ ___ ___ ___ ___ ___ ___
13 17 11 3 16 17 14 4

6. ___ ___ ___ ___ ___ ___ ___
9 4 8 15 17 14 4

Spellamadoodle

Skills:

Writing Spelling Words

Write each spelling word on the outline of the drawing. You may use the words more than once. For fun, decorate the drawing.

creature	feature	puncture	leisure
pleasure	natural	enough	physical
efficient	flexible	oily	turmoil

Skills:

Writing a List

An Unusual Animal

The duckbilled platypus is an unusual animal. It has webbed feet, a bill like a duck, and a body like a mammal. If you could bring together different parts of various animals, what kind of unusual animal might you build? Think of different animal parts like snouts, beaks, wings, hooves, tails, gills, and more! Be creative! "Construct" your animal below, listing all the parts it takes from different animals. Then give your new animal a name.

The name of my animal is

____

My animal is made up of the following parts:

____

____

____

____

____

____

Draw a picture of your unusual pet.

Unusual Animal Report

Skills:

Writing a Report

Now that you have "built" your unusual animal, write a report about it. Think about where your animal lives, what it eats, and what kind of home it has. Does your animal have any enemies? How does it defend itself? Use as many spelling words as you can.

creature	feature	puncture	leisure
pleasure	natural	enough	physical
efficient	flexible	oily	turmoil

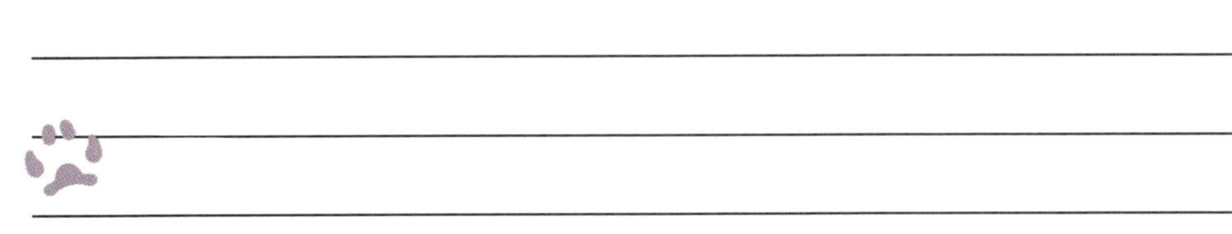

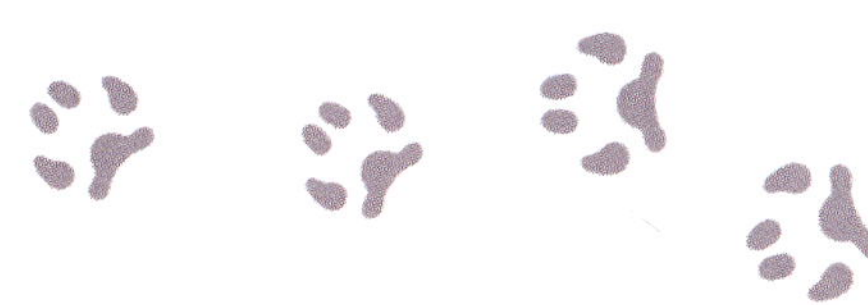

Edit Your Work

- ◯ I used complete sentences.
- ◯ I used correct spelling.
- ◯ I used correct capitalization and punctuation.

The Duckbilled Platypus

Find the correct answer. Fill in the circle.

1. Which sentence has the correct subject/verb agreement?
   - ◯ The zoo open at 10:00 a.m. on Saturdays.
   - ◯ Our class will meets in front of the school.
   - ◯ How many people fit on this bus?

2. Which sentence has the correct subject/verb agreement?
   - ◯ Platypuses close their eyes underwater.
   - ◯ The platypus are an unusual creature.
   - ◯ Its sharp leg spurs can punctures skin.

3. Which word means "great confusion"?
   - ◯ feature
   - ◯ leisure
   - ◯ turmoil

4. Which word is spelled correctly?
   - ◯ efficent
   - ◯ efficient
   - ◯ efficeint

Spelling Test

Ask someone to test you on the spelling words.

1. ____________________
2. ____________________
3. ____________________
4. ____________________
5. ____________________
6. ____________________
7. ____________________
8. ____________________
9. ____________________
10. ____________________
11. ____________________
12. ____________________

5. Write the sentence correctly.

   the platypus's owly hair is waterproof, which makes it an effcient swimmer

   ____

   ____

The Grand Canyon

The Grand Canyon in Arizona is one of the most famous natural wonders in the United States. The Grand Canyon was carved out by the action of the Colorado River. In other words, the river formed the canyon over millions of years by cutting through layers of different kinds of rock. Scientific opinion is that the deepest layers of rock are 2.5 billion years old.

Photo: National Park Service

The canyon has many layers of life, too. In some places, the upper edge is covered with forests or dotted with cactuses. There is no shortage of animals. Mule deer, bighorn sheep, bobcats, coyote, and bats make the canyon their home. Estimations are that there are about 300 species of birds. The unique pink rattlesnake and the white-tailed Kaibab squirrels are found only in this canyon.

Native Americans were the first to settle in the canyon. In 1540, Spanish explorers arrived. Then in 1869, Major John Wesley Powell traveled on the river through the canyon. After careful observation, Powell named it the "Grand Canyon." President Theodore Roosevelt visited the canyon in 1903. There was little argument when he named it a national park five years later. Today, the Grand Canyon does not have a shortage of visitors. It gets five million visitors a year!

Find It! Read the spelling words.
Check off the words you can find in the story.

☐ opinion	☐ appearance	☐ national	☐ argument
☐ shortage	☐ ordinary	☐ succession	☐ observation
☐ estimation	☐ action	☐ persuasion	☐ expression

How many spelling words did you find? _____

Skills:

Spelling Theme Vocabulary

Visual Memory

Suffixes of **–ion** and **–tion**

Spelling Practice

Read and Spell	Copy and Spell	Spell It Again!
1. opinion	______	______
2. appearance	______	______
3. national	______	______
4. argument	______	______
5. shortage	______	______
6. ordinary	______	______
7. succession	______	______
8. observation	______	______
9. estimation	______	______
10. action	______	______
11. persuasion	______	______
12. expression	______	______

Spell It Out

Skills:

Visual Memory

Recognizing Spelling Words

Circle the misspelled words in the sentences. Write them correctly on the lines.

1. In my upineon, the Grand Canyon is no ordinnare place to visit.

 ______________________ ______________________

2. The canyon is an espretion of America's nashunal beauty.

 ______________________ ______________________

3. For five years in sussession, there has been breaking acion in the rock layers.

 ______________________ ______________________

4. No persuation or arrgumint would have kept us away from the rim of the canyon!

 ______________________ ______________________

5. Scientific estimmasion is that there is no shortege of rock layers in the canyon.

 ______________________ ______________________

6. The apeerrance of a pink rattlesnake at the park was an exciting obsurvasion.

 ______________________ ______________________

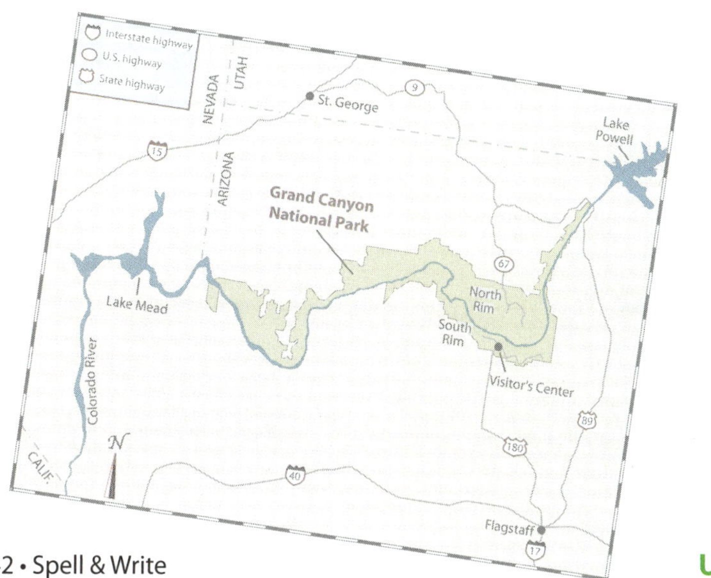

Skills:

Spelling Theme Vocabulary

Word Meaning

Writing Complete Sentences

What Does It Mean?

Write the letter of the definition that matches each spelling word.

_____	1. national	a.	the act of making a guess
_____	2. argument	b.	something that is done
_____	3. expression	c.	not having enough of something
_____	4. ordinary	d.	the ideas and beliefs you have about something
_____	5. opinion	e.	the act of making someone do or believe something
_____	6. succession	f.	the action of seeing or noticing
_____	7. shortage	g.	to do with, or belonging to, a nation as a whole
_____	8. persuasion	h.	average, not distinguished in any way
_____	9. appearance	i.	a number of things that follow one after the other in order
_____	10. estimation	j.	the act of disagreeing with someone
_____	11. observation	k.	the act of coming into view
_____	12. action	l.	the act of showing or representing feeling

Write a sentence using the spelling words *opinion* and *argument*.

____

____

Write a sentence using the spelling words *ordinary* and *observation*.

____

____

Amazing Adjectives

Skills:

Identifying Kinds of Adjectives

Adjectives describe nouns and pronouns.

- **An adjective can tell what kind, which one, or how many.**

Several pink rattlesnakes slept under that rock.

Several — how many; pink — what kind; that — which one

Circle all the adjectives in the following paragraphs. Hint: There are 25 adjectives!

Many people hike down into the Grand Canyon each year. Some parts of the canyon are accessible only by mule. Miles of challenging trails wind through this amazing park. There are nearly 1,500 species of plants growing here. It is also the cozy home to 300 species of birds, 88 species of mammals, and 58 species of reptiles. Imagine the incredible sights and sounds you might experience during your visit!

The Grand Canyon is immense. It covers a breathtaking 1,904 square miles. The Colorado River runs 277 miles through the canyon. People brave its dangerous rapids just for fun. If you are one of the five million tourists to visit the canyon this year, be sure to take many beautiful photographs to show your friends.

Skills:

Visual Sequencing

Recognizing Spelling Words

Word Search

Find and circle the spelling words. Words can go across, down, or diagonally.

opinion	appearance	national	argument
shortage	ordinary	succession	observation
estimation	action	persuasion	expression

Spellamadoodle

Skills:

Writing Spelling Words

Write each spelling word on the outline of the drawing. You may use the words more than once. For fun, decorate the drawing.

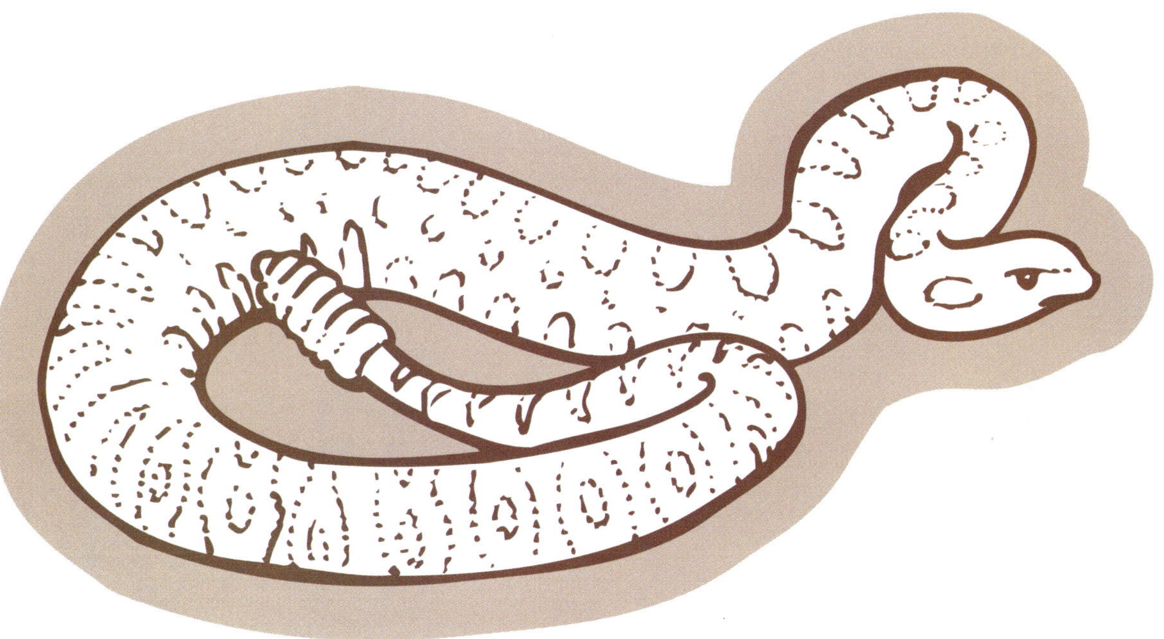

opinion	appearance	national	argument
shortage	ordinary	succession	observation
estimation	action	persuasion	expression

Skills:

Writing an Advertisement

Using Spelling Words in an Original Composition

Visit the Grand Canyon!

You have learned some amazing facts about the Grand Canyon. Use what you've learned to write an advertisement. Try to persuade people to visit this incredible national park. Use exciting, enticing adjectives to describe the canyon. Tell people what they might see and all the things they can do. Use as many spelling words as you can.

opinion	appearance	national	argument
shortage	ordinary	succession	observation
estimation	action	persuasion	expression

ADVERTISEMENT

Edit Your Work

- ❍ I used complete sentences.
- ❍ I used correct spelling.
- ❍ I used correct capitalization and punctuation.

A Day in the Canyon

Skills:
Writing a Journal Entry

You are visiting the Grand Canyon with your family. Today, you rode donkeys down to the inner canyon. You are camping there. Write a journal entry about your day. What did you see and hear? What did it feel like to ride a donkey down the treacherous trail? Were you scared? excited? What else happened?

The Grand Canyon

Find the correct answer. Fill in the circle.

1. Which sentence contains an adjective?
   - ❍ I love the layers of rock at the Grand Canyon.
   - ❍ Visitors can see animals and plants along the trails.
   - ❍ The beautiful Colorado River winds through the park.
2. Which sentence contains two adjectives?
   - ❍ The Grand Canyon has 300 species of colorful birds.
   - ❍ The Grand Canyon has 88 species of mammals.
   - ❍ The Grand Canyon is home to 58 species of reptiles.
3. Which of these is a definition for the word *succession*?
   - ❍ the act of disagreeing with someone
   - ❍ a number of things that follow one after another in order
   - ❍ the ideas and beliefs you have about something
4. Which word is spelled correctly?
   - ❍ argument
   - ❍ arguement
   - ❍ argeument

Spelling Test

Ask someone to test you on the spelling words.

1. ____________________
2. ____________________
3. ____________________
4. ____________________
5. ____________________
6. ____________________
7. ____________________
8. ____________________
9. ____________________
10. ____________________
11. ____________________
12. ____________________

5. Write the sentence correctly.

   it is my oppineon that the apearance of Grand Canyon Natonal Park is not oredinnary

   ____

   ____

Amazing Morse

Samuel Morse was born in Charlestown, Massachusetts, on April 27, 1791. In 1832, he became a painting and sculpture professor at the University of the City of New York. While on an ocean voyage, Morse discussed with his fellow passengers the idea of transmitting messages at great distances using electricity. The idea was brilliant. Over the next few years, Morse was persistent about creating this new device. After all, it was an ambitious project.

Finally, he finished his new invention. In 1844, the first official telegraph message was sent from Washington to Baltimore.

The telegraph would not have been as significant without the code Morse developed. The code is a series of dots and dashes equivalent to the letters of the alphabet. Dots are called "dits." Dashes are called "dahs." One sends messages by tapping out the letters using a telegraph key. The telegraph changed the taps into electric signals sent over telegraph wires. Morse code is still used today. Most people have heard of the distress signal S-O-S. The signal is sent as: dit dit dit, dah dah dah, dit dit dit.

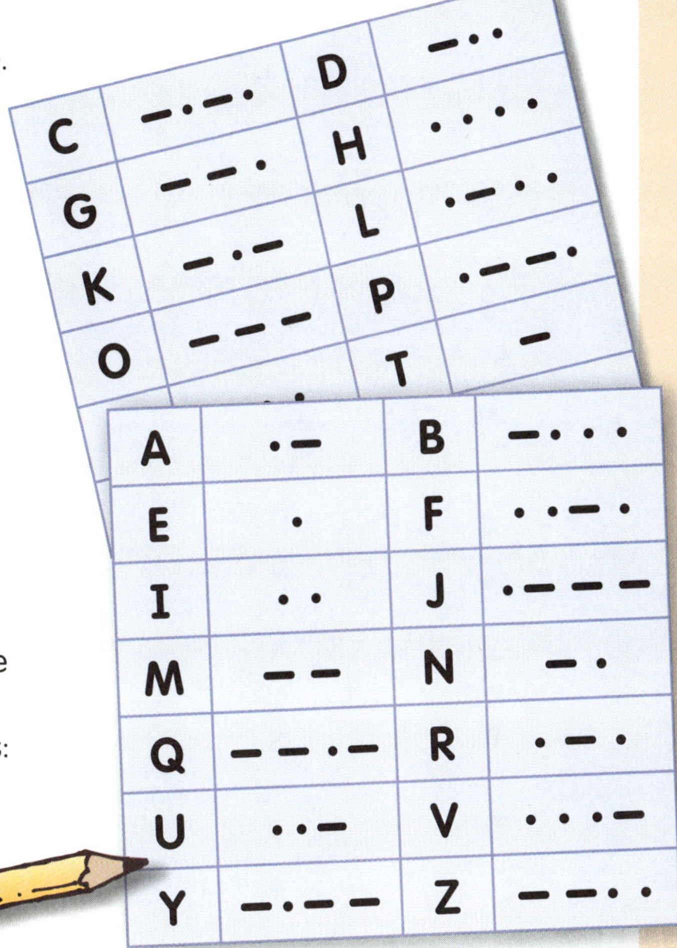

Find It!

Read the spelling words.
Check off the words you can find in the story.

☐ persistent	☐ equivalent	☐ brilliant	☐ significant
☐ attendant	☐ impatient	☐ ambitious	☐ ocean
☐ establish	☐ surely	☐ conversation	☐ official

How many spelling words did you find? _____

Skills:

Patterns of **–ent** and **–ant**

Spelling Theme Vocabulary

Visual Memory

Spelling Practice

Read and Spell	Copy and Spell	Spell It Again!
1. persistent	______________	______________
2. equivalent	______________	______________
3. brilliant	______________	______________
4. significant	______________	______________
5. attendant	______________	______________
6. impatient	______________	______________
7. ambitious	______________	______________
8. ocean	______________	______________
9. establish	______________	______________
10. surely	______________	______________
11. conversation	______________	______________
12. official	______________	______________

Word Study

Skills:

Visual Discrimination

Recognizing Adjectives

Circle the spelling words that could be used as adjectives.

brilliant	significant	impatient	surely
ocean	conversation	official	persistent
ambitious	equivalent	attendant	establish

Fill in the missing letters to make spelling words.

br ____ ll ____ ____ nt

establ ____ ____ ____

equiv ____ l ____ ____t

pers ____ st ____ ____ t

signif ____ c ____ ____ t

s ____ ____ ____ ly

oc ____ ____ n

att ____ nd ____ ____ t

offi ____ ____ ____ l

conversa ____ ____ ____ n

impa ____ ____ ____ nt

ambit ____ ____ ____ s

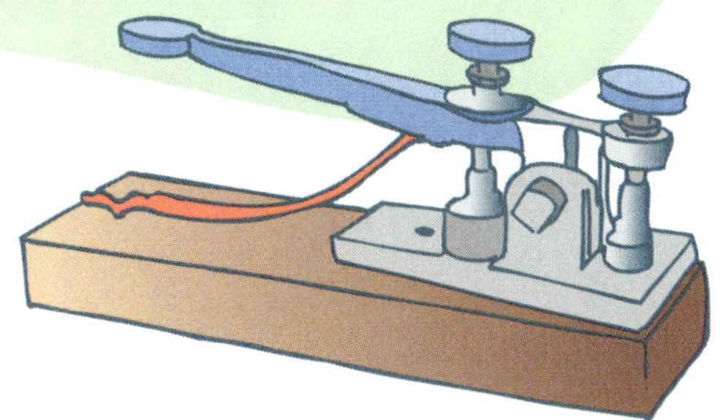

Skills:

Patterns of –**ent** and –**ant**

Spelling Theme Vocabulary

Visual Discrimination

Choose the Spelling

Circle the word in each row that is spelled correctly.

1.	ambishus	ambitious	ambitous
2.	oshun	osean	ocean
3.	convrsasion	conversation	convursateon
4.	surely	shurly	surrelly
5.	briliiant	brilleant	brilliant
6.	persistant	pursistint	persistent
7.	ophicial	official	oficcial
8.	eqwivalant	equivalent	equivelant
9.	establish	stablush	ustablich
10.	signifucent	signiffecant	significant
11.	impatient	impatent	impattient
12.	attendent	attendant	atendint

Fill in the endings of these spelling words.

ent
ant

persist ______ attend ______ brilli ______

equival ______ signific ______ impati ______

Comma Corrections

Skills:

Correcting for Commas

A **comma** is used to separate words in a series, equal adjectives, and long dependent clauses.

> We went to Boston, New York, and Philadelphia.
>
> The telegraph is an important, significant invention.
>
> While on an ocean voyage, Morse got a brilliant idea.

A **comma** is also used after introductory words and to set off the name of the person spoken to.

> Come here, Samuel, and listen to this.
>
> Yes, that is a brilliant idea!

Add commas where they are needed in each sentence.

1. Jenny what is Morse code for the signal S-O-S?
2. A series of small individual "dits" and "dahs" represent the alphabet.
3. Maya I'd like to send a message to Brian Tye and Serena.
4. Because of Morse code many significant messages have been sent.
5. Did you memorize the code for each letter Maile?
6. Yes Morse was a persisent ambitious person.
7. Listen Tom to this long message.
8. Do you understand all the dits dahs dots and dashes Tom?
9. As we listened to the message I began to understand a few words.
10. Because of the telegraph's importance Morse is a famous man.
11. No I don't think I can figure out this detailed complicated message.
12. Come here Justin and help me figure this out.

Skills:

Visual Sequencing

Recognizing Spelling Words

Word Search

Find and circle the spelling words. Words can go across, down, or diagonally.

persistent	equivalent	brilliant	significant
attendant	impatient	ambitious	ocean
establish	surely	conversation	official

S	I	G	N	I	F	I	C	A	N	T	V	W	C
U	A	N	T	C	I	F	E	L	Y	Z	L	O	D
O	K	H	S	I	L	B	A	T	S	E	N	S	T
I	M	P	A	T	I	E	N	T	M	V	O	O	N
T	Y	E	O	C	E	S	A	N	E	E	F	S	E
I	A	R	M	C	Z	O	M	R	E	L	F	Q	L
B	M	S	P	O	E	S	S	D	Z	Y	I	E	A
M	B	I	S	O	S	A	O	U	N	R	C	Y	V
A	I	S	Z	B	T	C	N	X	R	B	I	R	I
I	T	T	B	I	M	O	R	S	E	E	A	U	U
E	S	E	O	Z	U	N	L	I	S	H	L	S	Q
N	P	N	T	N	A	I	L	L	I	R	B	Y	E
A	A	T	T	E	N	D	A	N	T	T	T	B	Y
B	S	I	G	N	I	F	I	C	C	E	N	T	Y

Spellamadoodle

Skills:

Writing Spelling Words

Write each spelling word on the outline of the drawing. You may use the words more than once. For fun, decorate the drawing.

persistent	equivalent	brilliant	significant
attendant	impatient	ambitious	ocean
establish	surely	conversation	official

Skills:

Learning Morse Code

Solving a Puzzle

Crack the Code

Study the Morse code alphabet. Then use it to figure out the mystery message below.

A	• —	B	— • • •	C	— • — •	D	— • •
E	•	F	• • — •	G	— — •	H	• • • •
I	• •	J	• — — —	K	— • —	L	• — • •
M	— —	N	— •	O	— — —	P	• — — •
Q	— — • —	R	• — •	S	• • •	T	—
U	• • —	V	• • • —	W	• — —	X	— • • —
Y	— • — —	Z	— — • •				

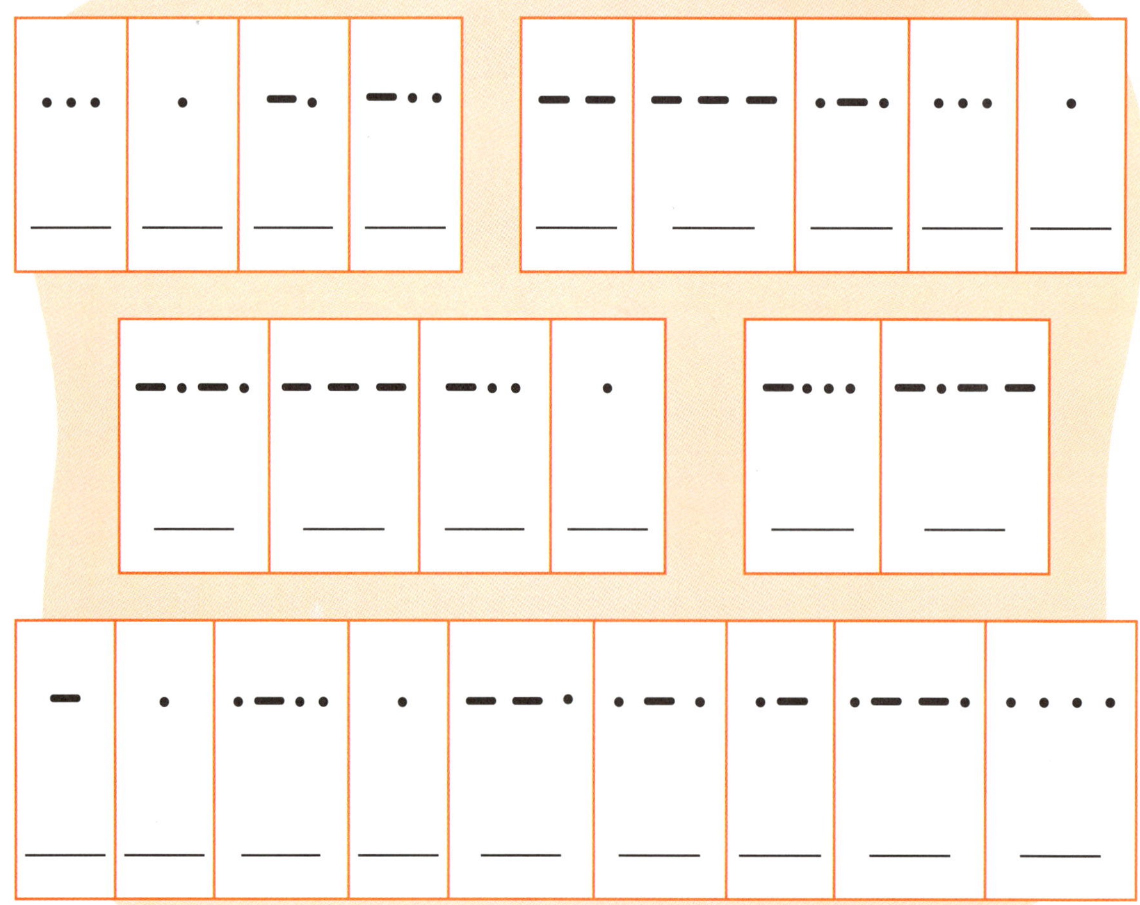

Morse Code Message

Skills:

Writing a Morse Code Message

Now that you know Morse code, send your own message! Think of a friend to whom you'd like to send a message. Fill in each box with a letter from the code on page 60. Draw a vertical line between boxes to separate words. Then give your message to a friend to solve!

____	____	____	____	____	____	____	____

____	____	____	____	____	____	____	____

____	____	____	____	____	____	____	____

____	____	____	____	____	____	____	____

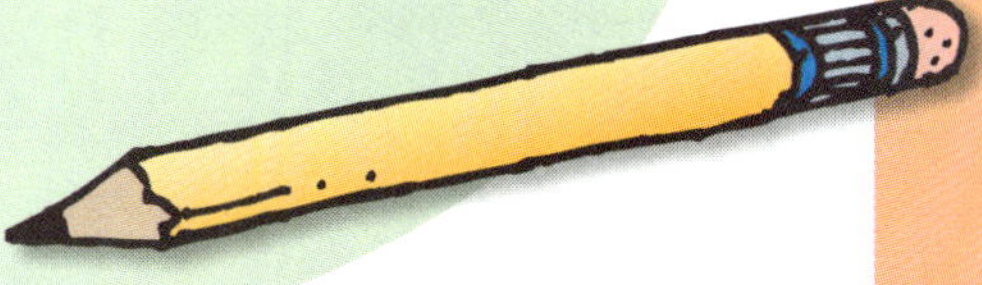

Amazing Morse

Find the correct answer. Fill in the circle.

1. Which sentence uses capital letters and commas correctly?
   - ❍ Yes Samuel morse taught college in new York.
   - ❍ Yes, Samuel Morse taught college in New York.
   - ❍ Yes, samuel, Morse taught College in new york.
2. Which sentence uses capital letters and commas correctly?
   - ❍ In March, I sent twenty Morse code messages to Mr. Justice.
   - ❍ in march i sent twenty morse code Messages to mr. Justice.
   - ❍ In March I sent twenty Morse Code Messages to Mr. justice.
3. Which word does not describe Samuel Morse?
   - ❍ brilliant
   - ❍ impatient
   - ❍ persistent
4. Which word is spelled correctly?
   - ❍ offical
   - ❍ officail
   - ❍ official

Spelling Test

Ask someone to test you on the spelling words.

1. ______________________
2. ______________________
3. ______________________
4. ______________________
5. ______________________
6. ______________________
7. ______________________
8. ______________________
9. ______________________
10. ______________________
11. ______________________
12. ______________________

5. Write the sentence correctly.

we can establlush a good convursasion using the offisail morse code

____

____

Race of Mercy

The winter of 1925 was bitterly cold in Nome, Alaska. In January, several children became very ill. Doctors were doubtful that the children would live. Without medicine, they were powerless. The serum was in Anchorage, nearly a thousand miles away. A vicious storm was starting. The rugged wilderness was pounded by winds, and temperatures plunged to 40 degrees below zero. The most sensible way to send the serum was by dog sled relay.

Within hours of the call for help, a dog sled musher and his dog team left Anchorage. They carried precious medicine wrapped in furs. Twenty-one heroic mushers took part in the relay. Six days later, the final team finished the race of mercy. Curious townspeople stared in amazement as a tireless Siberian husky named Balto loped into view. The medicine had arrived in time. The grateful children were saved.

Numerous newspapers around the world carried the story of the successful rescue. Balto and his brave team were famous. A statue of Balto was placed in New York City's Central Park. And all the lovable canine heroes spent the rest of their lives in comfort in special quarters at the Cleveland Zoo.

Find It!

Read the spelling words.
Check off the words you can find in the story.

- [ ] lovable
- [ ] sensible
- [ ] vicious
- [ ] precious
- [ ] amazement
- [ ] successful
- [ ] doubtful
- [ ] powerless
- [ ] tireless
- [ ] curious
- [ ] numerous
- [ ] grateful

How many spelling words did you find? _____

Skills:

Spelling Words with Suffixes **–able**, **–ible**, **–ous**, **–ment**, **–ful**, **–less**

Spelling Theme Vocabulary

Visual Memory

Spelling Practice

Read and Spell	Copy and Spell	Spell It Again!
1. lovable	______	______
2. sensible	______	______
3. vicious	______	______
4. precious	______	______
5. amazement	______	______
6. successful	______	______
7. doubtful	______	______
8. powerless	______	______
9. tireless	______	______
10. curious	______	______
11. numerous	______	______
12. grateful	______	______

Find the Words

Fill in the blanks with words from the spelling list.

1. They watched in ________________ as Balto ran into view.
2. Without medicine, the doctors felt ________________ against the disease.
3. Hardly resting, a ________________ dog team carried the medicine.
4. These sweet, ________________ dogs are everybody's best friend.
5. A violent, ________________ storm almost kept the dogs away.
6. The children were very ________________ for the medicine.
7. Many were ________________ that the dangerous mission would be ________________.
8. Newspapers around the world carried ________________ stories of bravery.

Fill in the suffixes to make spelling words. Hint: You will have to drop the silent *e* for one of the words.

able	ible	ment
ful	less	ous

sens ______	lov ______	amaze ______
vici ______	grate ______	numer ______
doubt ______	tire ______	success ______
curi ______	power ______	preci ______

Skills:

Spelling Words with Suffixes **–able**, **–ible**, **–ous**, **–ment**, **–ful**, **–less**

Spelling Theme Vocabulary

Visual Memory

Using Context Clues to Find Missing Words

Skills:

Spelling
Theme
Vocabulary

Recognizing Antonyms and Synonyms

Word Meanings

Write the spelling word that is an antonym (the opposite) for each of the following words:

hateful ______________________

defeated ______________________

few ______________________

powerful ______________________

sure ______________________

Write the spelling word that is a synonym (the same) for each of the following words:

ferocious ______________________

thankful ______________________

energetic ______________________

reasonable ______________________

interested ______________________

lovable	sensible	vicious	precious
amazement	successful	doubtful	powerless
tireless	curious	numerous	grateful

Comma Challenge

Skills:

Correcting for Commas

- A comma is used to separate words in a series; equal adjectives; long dependent clauses; the day and year in a date; and the city and state, province, or country.
- A comma is also used after introductory words and to set off the name of the person spoken to.

Add commas where they are needed in each sentence.

1. The dog team traveled from Nome Alaska to Anchorage Alaska.
2. Jess did you see those amazing tireless dogs?
3. Because of the storm people doubted the dogs would make it.
4. Dogs mushers and precious medicine made the journey.
5. Yes Wendy the dogs retired at the zoo in Cleveland Ohio.
6. Well I'm not sure of Balto's age during the relay.
7. He was a loved admired hero Shawna.
8. A statue of Balto stands in Central Park in New York City New York.
9. I found out about this story on Tuesday December 12 2004.
10. No Manuel I can't lend you the book until next week.
11. While the wild cold winds blew the temperature dropped.
12. Have you ever been to Anchorage Alaska Tonya?

Skills:

Visual Discrimination

Using Spelling Words

Secret Code

Write the letter that stands for each number to discover six of the spelling words.

a	b	c	d	e	f	g	i	l	m	n	o	p	r	s	t	u	v	w
1	2	3	4	5	6	7	8	9	10	11	12	13	14	15	16	17	18	19

1. ___ ___ ___ ___ ___ ___ ___
18 8 3 8 12 17 15

2. ___ ___ ___ ___ ___ ___ ___
3 17 14 8 12 17 15

3. ___ ___ ___ ___ ___ ___ ___ ___
13 14 5 3 8 12 17 15

4. ___ ___ ___ ___ ___ ___ ___ ___
11 17 10 5 14 12 17 15

5. ___ ___ ___ ___ ___ ___ ___ ___ ___
13 12 19 5 14 9 5 15 15

6. ___ ___ ___ ___ ___ ___ ___ ___ ___ ___
15 17 3 3 5 15 15 6 17 9

Spellamadoodle

Write each spelling word on the outline of the drawing. You may use the words more than once. For fun, decorate the drawing.

lovable	sensible	vicious	precious
amazement	successful	doubtful	powerless
tireless	curious	numerous	grateful

Skills:

Writing Spelling Words

Skills:

Writing a Newspaper Article

Using Spelling Words in an Original Composition

Balto, the Hero!

It's winter 1925. You are a newspaper reporter in Nome, Alaska. You have been asked to write an article about the "race of mercy." You are with the townspeople in the bitter cold, waiting for the dog teams to arrive. Suddenly, you hear a cheer go up from the crowd! Write a newspaper article describing in detail what you saw, heard, and experienced as the teams pulled in. Use as many spelling words as you can.

lovable	sensible	vicious	precious
amazement	successful	doubtful	powerless
tireless	curious	numerous	grateful

OUR FEATURE ARTICLE

THE DAILY GRIND

SUNDAY EDITION

Animal Heroes

Skills:

Writing a Creative Story

Have you ever heard of other animal heroes besides Balto? Cats have been known to warn their owners of a burning house. Dogs have found lost people just by scent. Write a story about an animal that did a heroic deed. What happened, and how did the animal save the day?

Edit Your Work

- ○ I used complete sentences.
- ○ I used correct spelling.
- ○ I used correct capitalization and punctuation.

Race of Mercy

Find the correct answer. Fill in the circle.

1. Which sentence uses commas correctly?
   - ❍ No, Jamie, I didn't read the story of Balto.
   - ❍ No Jamie, I didn't read the story of Balto.
   - ❍ No, Jamie I didn't read the story of Balto.

2. Which sentence uses commas correctly?
   - ❍ On May 13 2004 my family moved to, Anchorage, Alaska.
   - ❍ On May 13, 2004, my family moved to Anchorage, Alaska.
   - ❍ On May, 13, 2004 my family moved to Anchorage Alaska.

3. Which word is an antonym for *vicious*?
   - ❍ curious
   - ❍ grateful
   - ❍ lovable

4. Which word is spelled correctly?
   - ❍ doutful
   - ❍ doubtful
   - ❍ doubtfull

Spelling Test

Ask someone to test you on the spelling words.

1. ____________________
2. ____________________
3. ____________________
4. ____________________
5. ____________________
6. ____________________
7. ____________________
8. ____________________
9. ____________________
10. ____________________
11. ____________________
12. ____________________

5. Write the sentence correctly.

the preshious serum brought greatfull smiles to numorious children in Alaska

____

____

The Olympic Flame

The opening ceremony of the Olympic games is always exciting. The athletes of Greece march into the stadium first, in honor of the original games held in ancient Greece. The most moving moment of the opening ceremony is the lighting of the Olympic flame.

A new flame is started in the ancient Olympic stadium in Olympia, Greece, for each Olympics. A mirror is used to concentrate the rays of the sun to start the fire. Runners carry a portable, lighted torch throughout Greece. If overland routes are inconvenient, the flame is taken to the host country by airplane. Runners are chosen to transport the flame in a torch relay to the stadium. Most runners carry the flame on foot. Participants occasionally ride horses or ski as they carry the torch.

The final independent runner carries the torch into the stadium and circles the track. That runner then lights a huge kettle, called a "cauldron." The audience reacts immediately to this moment. A huge round of applause echoes throughout the stadium. People tend to underestimate the flame's ability to keep on burning. In reality, the flame burns constantly throughout the games. Then, during the closing ceremony, the flame is extinguished. The immortal symbol of the Olympics, however, burns on in people's memories.

Find It! Read the spelling words.
Check off the words you can find in the story.

- [ ] independent
- [ ] inconvenient
- [ ] immortal
- [ ] immediate
- [ ] underneath
- [ ] underestimate
- [ ] uncertain
- [ ] unreliable
- [ ] enact
- [ ] react
- [ ] transport
- [ ] portable

How many spelling words did you find? ______

Skills:

Spelling Words with Prefixes **un–**, **in–**, **im–**, and **under–**

Root Words **act** and **port**

Spelling Theme Vocabulary

Visual Memory

Spelling Practice

Read and Spell	Copy and Spell	Spell It Again!
1. independent		
2. inconvenient		
3. immortal		
4. immediate		
5. underneath		
6. underestimate		
7. uncertain		
8. unreliable		
9. enact		
10. react		
11. transport		
12. portable		

Search and Spell

Circle the word in each row that is spelled correctly.

1.	imorttal	immoretal	immortal
2.	incunveniant	innconvenent	inconvenient
3.	transport	transsporte	trenspart
4.	undrneeth	underneath	underrnethe
5.	react	reeacte	reackt
6.	unsertan	uncertain	uncertine
7.	portible	poretuble	portable
8.	innact	enact	enacte
9.	immediate	imeddiat	emmedeate
10.	unnrelible	unreliuble	unreliable
11.	independant	indeppendint	independent
12.	underestimet	underestimate	undrestimmate

Circle the misspelled words in the sentences. Write them correctly on the lines.

1. The imeddiate response caused us to reeact.

   ____

2. Many eager people transporte the porteible torch.

   ____

3. Theodosius was uncertine whether he should innact the games.

   ____

4. No one should underestimiate the imorttal god Zeus.

   ____

Skills:

Spelling Words with Prefixes **un–**, **in–**, **im–**, and **under–**

Root Words **act** and **port**

Spelling Theme Vocabulary

Visual Discrimination

Skills:

Visual Memory

Word Meaning

Vocabulary Match

Write the missing part of each spelling word. Then write the letter of the definition that matches each spelling word.

_____	1. re __________	a. to think that something is not as good as it really is
_____	2. __________ estimate	b. taking place or done at once
_____	3. __________ able	c. not accessible or handy
_____	4. __________ mortal	d. to respond to something that happens
_____	5. __________ dependent	e. not sure about something
_____	6. en __________	f. not dependent on others
_____	7. __________ certain	g. to make into law
_____	8. trans __________	h. not dependable or trusted
_____	9. __________ mediate	i. living or lasting forever
_____	10. __________ neath	j. to move from one place to another
_____	11. __________ reliable	k. able to be carried or moved easily
_____	12. __________ convenient	l. under or below

Tricky Titles

Skills:

Identifying and Punctuating Titles

Writing Complete Sentences

Titles of books, movies, plays, magazines, songs, stories, etc., are treated in specific ways.

Capitalize the first word, the last word, and every important word in between.

Stories of the Old West

When you write by hand, underline the titles of books, movies, and television programs, and the names of newspapers and magazines.

New York Times (newspaper) Survivor (television show)

Use quotation marks around the titles of stories, magazine articles, songs, and poems.

"America the Beautiful" (song) "On the Pulse of Morning" (poem)

Rewrite each sentence correctly. Use correct punctuation.

1. Robert Frost's poem fire and ice is one of my favorites.

____

____

2. We get a boston globe newspaper every morning.

____

____

3. Mrs. Healy assigned island of the blue dolphins for a book report.

____

____

4. We sang the star spangled banner in the school concert.

____

____

5. Let's go see the movie the hunchback of notre dame on Saturday.

____

____

Skills:

Using Context Clues to Find Missing Words

Writing Spelling Words

Olympic Torch

Fill in the blanks with the spelling words. Use each word only once. You will not use one word.

independent	inconvenient	immortal	immediate
underneath	underestimate	uncertain	unreliable
enact	react	transport	portable

How would you ____________________ if someone said you could carry the Olympic torch? The ancient Greeks believed the Olympic games pleased the ____________________ god Zeus. Who would be pleased if you were involved?

Do not ____________________ the importance of carrying the Olympic torch. It is an honor! The torch carrier cannot be ____________________ about his or her role. The person cannot be ____________________ either. Some run with the torch. If running is ____________________, the torch travels by plane. Today's ____________________ torch is easy to ____________________ from place to place.

Seeing the torch go by brings ____________________ excitement and pride to onlookers. At the end of its journey, the torch arrives in the city hosting that year's Olympic games. There, the last ____________________ runner lights a huge cauldron, which burns bright throughout the games. Never forget, ____________________ all the glitz and glamour of the Olympic games is a long proud history of the ancient flame.

Spellamadoodle

Skills:

Writing Spelling Words

Write each spelling word on the outline of the drawing. You may use the words more than once. For fun, decorate the drawing.

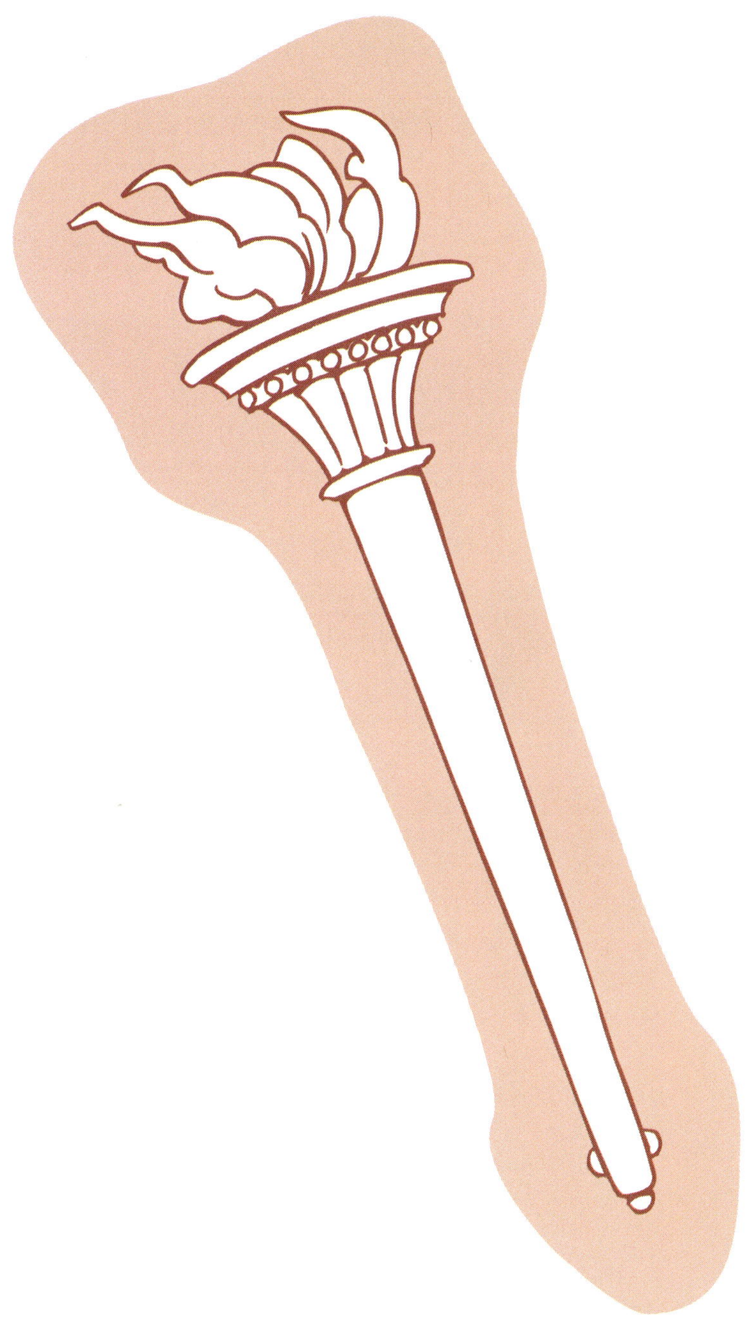

independent	inconvenient	immortal	immediate
underneath	underestimate	uncertain	unreliable
enact	react	transport	portable

Skills:

Using Spelling Words in an Acrostic Poem

Poetry Time

Create an acrostic poem. Write a word or phrase that starts with each letter in the topic word. Use a dictionary and the words in the article to help you.

THE OLYMPIC

F ______________________________

L ______________________________

A ______________________________

M ______________________________

E ______________________________

Carrying the Torch

Skills:

Writing a Friendly Letter

You have been asked to carry the Olympic torch through your hometown or city. What do you think it will be like? Will crowds cheer for you? How will you feel? Write a letter to a friend, telling about your experience carrying the Olympic torch.

____

________________________,

____

____

____

____

____

____

____

____

____

____

Your friend,

____

Edit Your Work

- ◯ I used complete sentences.
- ◯ I used correct spelling.
- ◯ I used correct capitalization and punctuation.

The Olympic Flame

Find the correct answer. Fill in the circle.

1. Which magazine article title is written correctly?
   - ○ English: why we should study the Language
   - ○ "English: Why We Should Study the Language"
   - ○ English: Why We Should Study The Language
2. Which book title is written correctly?
   - ○ Tales Of A Fourth-Grade Nothing
   - ○ "Tales of a Fourth-grade Nothing"
   - ○ *Tales of a Fourth-Grade Nothing*
3. Which word means "not dependable or trusted"?
   - ○ uncertain
   - ○ unreliable
   - ○ inconvenient
4. Which word is spelled correctly?
   - ○ immediate
   - ○ immeidate
   - ○ immeidiate

Spelling Test

Ask someone to test you on the spelling words.

1. ______
2. ______
3. ______
4. ______
5. ______
6. ______
7. ______
8. ______
9. ______
10. ______
11. ______
12. ______

5. Write the sentence correctly.

it's unconveniant for me to transspert that poretible torch imediately

______

______

Inuit Snowhouses

The geography and geology of the Arctic Circle make it a tough place to call home. In the winter, the nights lengthen until the sun barely shines. In the extreme north, the ground is permanently frozen. The hardy Inuit are the native people of northern Alaska, Canada, and Greenland. Traditionally, they hunted Arctic animals for food, especially caribou, seals, and whales. The Inuit used animal skins for clothing and for shelter.

Most traditional Inuit families had both a summer and a winter home. During the summer, many Inuit lived in tents covered with caribou or sealskins.

In the winter, some Inuit built sod houses. Other Inuit built snowhouses, or igloos. These dome-shaped shelters provided refuge from freezing temperatures.

Inuit workers could construct a snowhouse in about two hours. To begin, they cut hard-packed snow into blocks. The blocks were from 2 to 3 feet long and 1 to 2 feet wide. Next, the blocks were stacked together perfectly into a spiral. The spiral was wound upward in smaller and smaller circles to form the dome-shaped home. On top of the dome, a hole was cut out to provide fresh air. Finally, the workers dug an entrance tunnel to the snowhouse.

Today, most Inuit live in modern housing. But the tradition of building snowhouses is still passed down from one generation to another.

Find It! Read the spelling words.
Check off the words you can find in the story.

- [ ] geography
- [ ] geology
- [ ] geologist
- [ ] permanently
- [ ] especially
- [ ] immediately
- [ ] temporarily
- [ ] perfectly
- [ ] sincerely
- [ ] lengthen
- [ ] strengthen
- [ ] frighten

How many spelling words did you find? _____

Skills:

Spelling Words with Suffixes –**ly** and –**en**

Root Word **geo**

Spelling Theme Vocabulary

Visual Memory

Spelling Practice

Read and Spell	Copy and Spell	Spell It Again!
1. geography	____________	____________
2. geology	____________	____________
3. geologist	____________	____________
4. permanently	____________	____________
5. especially	____________	____________
6. immediately	____________	____________
7. temporarily	____________	____________
8. perfectly	____________	____________
9. sincerely	____________	____________
10. lengthen	____________	____________
11. strengthen	____________	____________
12. frighten	____________	____________

Crossword Challenge

Complete the crossword puzzle using words from the spelling list.

geography	geology	geologist	permanently
especially	immediately	temporarily	perfectly
sincerely	lengthen	strengthen	frighten

Across

1. with honesty and truth
3. to scare
6. flawlessly
7. for only a short time
8. the study of the Earth's layers of soil and rock
9. to make longer
10. to make stronger
12. at once; without delay

Down

2. more than usually; particularly
4. someone who studies the formations of the Earth
5. for a long time; indefinitely
11. the study of the Earth's people, resources, climate, and physical features

Skills:

Spelling Words with Suffixes **–ly** and **–en**

Root Word **geo**

Spelling Theme Vocabulary

Visual Discrimination

Skills:

Spelling Words with Suffixes –**ly** and –**en**

Root Word **geo**

Spelling Theme Vocabulary

Visual Memory

Spelling Words in Context

Spell Check

Circle the 12 misspelled words in the following paragraphs. Write the words correctly on the lines. All but one are spelling words.

Alana wants to be a giollogist when she grows up. How does she know? She loves to study geollojy. She also was sinseerly interested in jeography. Alana is espesally motivated to go to the Grand Canyon. Here she can strenthin her knowledge of earth's fascinating rock layers. The rocks at the bottom of the Grand Canyon may be more than 2 billion years old!

Alana and her friend Joey have planned a purffectly wonderful trip to the canyon. Temperarely, they will stay in a hotel on the South Rim. Then they will take a mule ride all the way down to the inner canyon. Some say this is a scary experience, but it takes a lot to friten Alana! Imeddiatly after arriving in the inner canyon, she and Joey will set up camp. Alana wants to lenthen their stay by another week by taking a rafting trip down the Colorado River. How does that sound for exciting?

1. ____________	5. ____________	9. ____________
2. ____________	6. ____________	10. ____________
3. ____________	7. ____________	11. ____________
4. ____________	8. ____________	12. ____________

Picking Prepositions

Skills:

Identifying and Using Prepositions

Writing Complete Sentences

A preposition is used to show the relationship of a noun or pronoun to another word in the sentence. Here are some common prepositions:

about	behind	during	inside	through
above	below	for	of	to
after	between	from	off	under
at	down	in	on	with

Circle the preposition or prepositions in each sentence.

1. Bianca said it was warm inside the igloo.

2. We should lengthen the space needed for the entrance.

3. Stuff the cracks between the blocks with snow.

4. You can cut through the snow to make blocks.

5. Let's build a snowman behind the igloo.

6. You may put my cap on the snowman's head.

7. We can dig another entrance to the igloo under the wall.

8. After the sun sets, we will light an oil lamp to keep warm.

Skills:

Visual Sequencing

Recognizing Spelling Words

Word Search

Find and circle the spelling words. Words can go across, down, or diagonally.

geography	geology	geologist	permanently
especially	immediately	temporarily	perfectly
sincerely	lengthen	strengthen	frighten

Spellamadoodle

Skills:

Writing Spelling Words

Write each spelling word on the outline of the drawing. You may use the words more than once. For fun, decorate the drawing.

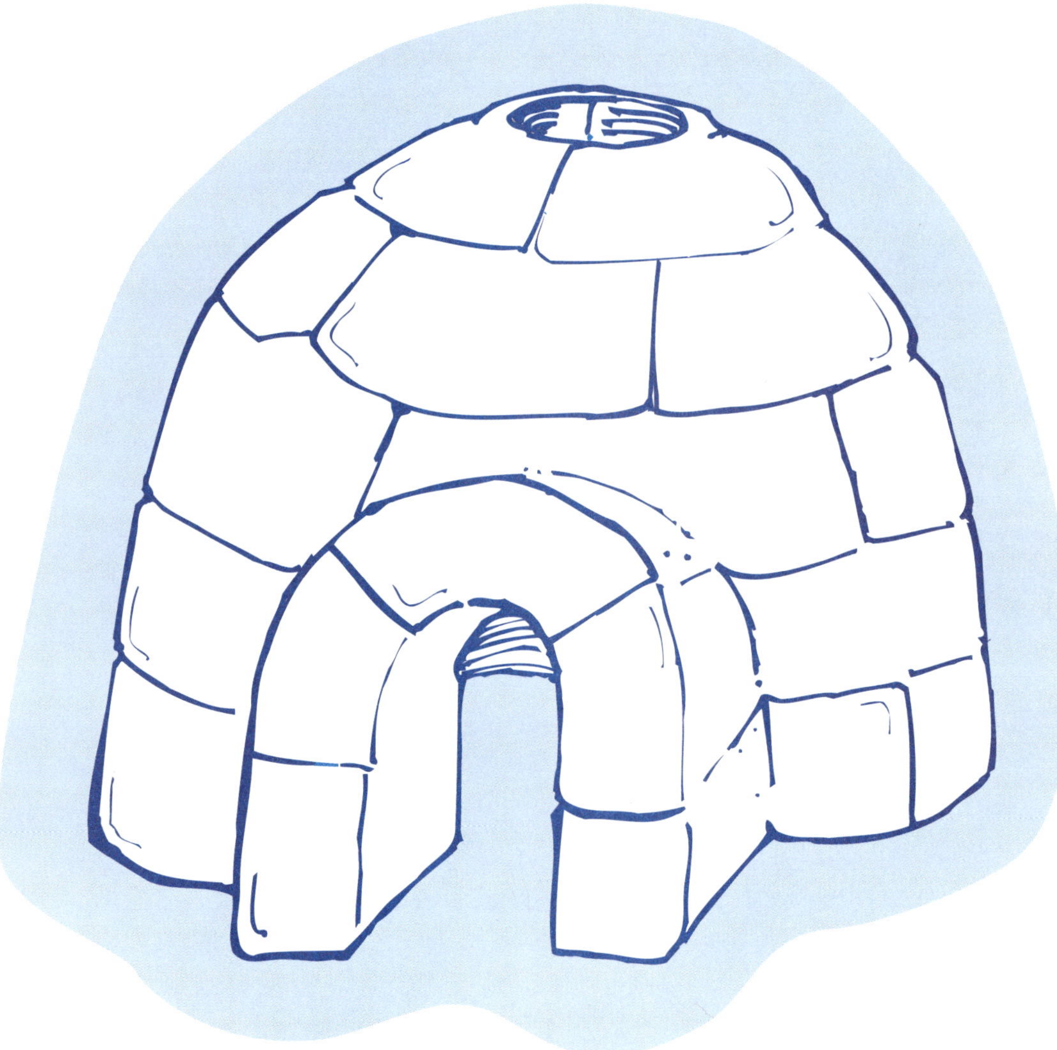

geography	geology	geologist	permanently
especially	immediately	temporarily	perfectly
sincerely	lengthen	strengthen	frighten

Skills:

Writing a How-to

Building an Igloo

Writing how to do something may not be as easy as you think! Instructions should be brief and to the point. They should also be written in order, step by step. Go back to the article and read how to build an igloo. Rewrite the paragraph as numbered steps below.

1. ____

2. ____

3. ____

4. ____

5. ____

Interview an Inuit

Skills:

Writing Interview Questions and Answers

What do you think it would be like to live like a traditional Inuit with an igloo as your home? Pretend you are a reporter, and you are going to interview an Inuit. Ask about his or her daily life, including hunting, home and family life, clothing, and more. Write both your questions and the Inuit's answers in a question-and-answer format.

Q:

A:

Q:

A:

Q:

A:

Inuit Snowhouses

Find the correct answer. Fill in the circle.

1. In which sentence is the preposition underlined?
   - ❍ Marco crawled into the dome-shaped igloo.
   - ❍ Marco crawled into the dome-shaped igloo.
   - ❍ Marco crawled into the dome-shaped igloo.
2. In which sentence is the preposition underlined?
   - ❍ Our sled raced quickly down the hill.
   - ❍ Our sled raced quickly down the hill.
   - ❍ Our sled raced quickly down the hill.
3. Which word means "the study of the Earth's layers of rock and soil"?
   - ❍ geology
   - ❍ geologist
   - ❍ geography
4. Which word is spelled correctly?
   - ❍ especielly
   - ❍ especially
   - ❍ especailly

Spelling Test

Ask someone to test you on the spelling words.

1. ______________________
2. ______________________
3. ______________________
4. ______________________
5. ______________________
6. ______________________
7. ______________________
8. ______________________
9. ______________________
10. ______________________
11. ______________________
12. ______________________

5. Write the sentence correctly.

   the geugrafy and geollogey of the Arctic Circle might frigten people who want to live there

   ____

   ____

Microgravity

Photo: NASA

Have you ever seen astronauts orbiting Earth in a spacecraft? They appear weightless. That means gravity is nonexistent, right? Nonsense! The gravitation in orbit is slightly less than the gravitation on Earth. Because of the spacecraft's tremendous speed, the Earth's surface curves away as the spacecraft falls toward it. This free fall seems to eliminate the weight of everything inside the spacecraft. For this reason, the condition is sometimes called "weightlessness," but the more correct term is "microgravity."

Astronauts react to microgravity in several ways. In the first few days of a mission, about half of the astronauts suffer from

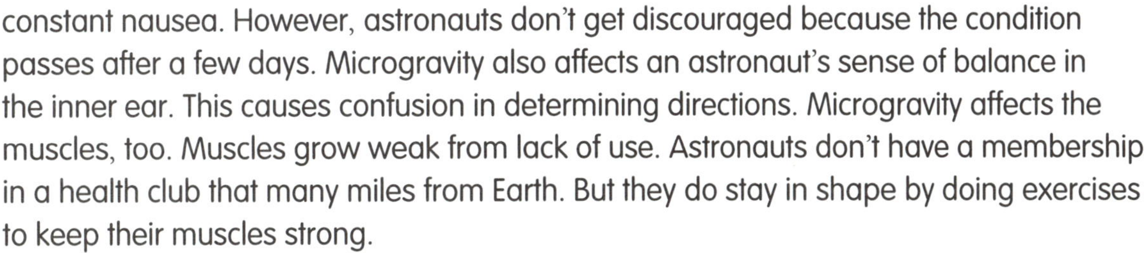

constant nausea. However, astronauts don't get discouraged because the condition passes after a few days. Microgravity also affects an astronaut's sense of balance in the inner ear. This causes confusion in determining directions. Microgravity affects the muscles, too. Muscles grow weak from lack of use. Astronauts don't have a membership in a health club that many miles from Earth. But they do stay in shape by doing exercises to keep their muscles strong.

People may disagree on which term to use for the condition of weightlessness. But every citizen in the U.S. agrees on one thing. It is an awesome sight to see astronauts floating freely in space.

Find It! Read the spelling words.
Check off the words you can find in the story.

- [ ] citizenship
- [ ] partnership
- [ ] ownership
- [ ] championship
- [ ] membership
- [ ] dishonest
- [ ] discourage
- [ ] disagree
- [ ] disgrace
- [ ] nonsense
- [ ] nonexistent
- [ ] nonfiction

How many spelling words did you find? _____

Skills:

Spelling Words with the Suffix –**ship** and the Prefixes **non**– and **dis**–

Spelling Theme Vocabulary

Visual Memory

Spelling Practice

Read and Spell	Copy and Spell	Spell It Again!
1. citizenship	____________	____________
2. partnership	____________	____________
3. ownership	____________	____________
4. championship	____________	____________
5. membership	____________	____________
6. dishonest	____________	____________
7. discourage	____________	____________
8. disagree	____________	____________
9. disgrace	____________	____________
10. nonsense	____________	____________
11. nonexistent	____________	____________
12. nonfiction	____________	____________

Making Spelling Words

Read the meanings of the prefixes and suffix. Then fill in the blanks to make spelling words. Match each word to its meaning by writing the corresponding letter on the line.

dis = not; opposite   non = not   ship = state or quality of

a. ________ honest   ________ final game of a series that decides the winner

b. citizen ________   ________ not fiction; not made up

c. ________ existent   ________ does not exist

d. ________ fiction   ________ something that is silly or has no meaning

e. owner ________   ________ two or more people who do something together

f. member ________   ________ to not agree

g. ________ courage   ________ the state of being a citizen

h. ________ sense   ________ belonging to a group

i. partner ________   ________ causing shame or disapproval

j. ________ agree   ________ the quality of owning something

k. champion ________   ________ to encourage someone not to do something

l. ________ grace   ________ opposite of honest

Skills:

Spelling Words with the Suffix **–ship** and the Prefixes **non–** and **dis–**

Spelling Theme Vocabulary

Visual Memory

Word Meaning

Skills:

Spelling Words with the Suffix **–ship** and the Prefixes **non–** and **dis–**

Spelling Theme Vocabulary

Visual Memory

Spelling Words in Context

Which Spelling?

Circle the correct spelling.

1. Is gravity **nonexistiant**/**nonexistent** in space?
2. It's **disonnest**/**dishonest** to copy a friend's homework assignment.
3. The **championship**/**champeonsip** game is this weekend.
4. I should **discorege**/**discourage** you from joining the club.
5. Most books about gravity are **nonfiction**/**nonfichon**.
6. My **membership**/**membrshipe** is important to the science club.
7. It's no **discrase**/**disgrace** that you didn't make the team.
8. I now have complete **onership**/**ownership** of my new car.
9. The two scientists formed a **partnership**/**parttnerchip**.
10. We thought the whole movie was **nonsense**/**nonesens**.
11. Mia might **dissagre**/**disagree** with that opinion.
12. Dan is proud of his dual English-American **citesinship**/**citizenship**.

Colons in Letters

Skills:

Using Colons and Commas

Colons are used:

• to separate the hour and minutes in time	10:30 7:15
• after the greeting in a business letter	Dear Ms. Stamp:
• before writing a list	Bring the following: pencils paper erasers

Punctuate the following business letter. Use colons and commas where needed.

June 14 2005

Mr. Jon Little
3321 First Ave.
Whittier CA 90817

Dear Mr. Little

I am pleased to hear that you will be speaking at our meeting on July 22 2005. The meeting begins at 1 30 p.m. We would like you to join us for lunch at 12 00 p.m.

On that day, please bring the following with you

slide presentation
speakers
handouts
notebooks
any additional materials you need

We are looking forward to seeing you! I will be available between 7 30 a.m. and 4 30 p.m. if you have any further questions.

Sincerely

Rita Hernandez

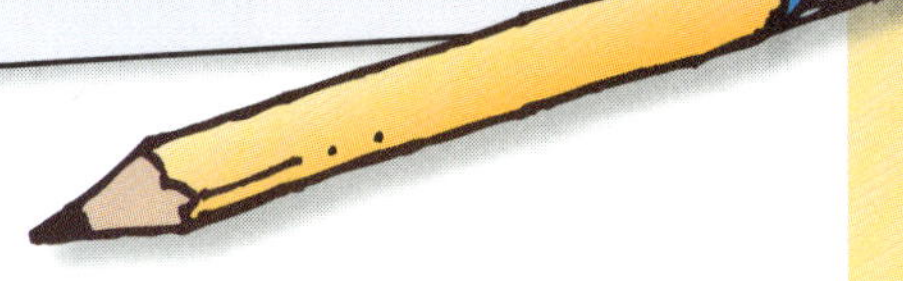

Skills:

Visual Discrimination

Using Spelling Words

Secret Code

Write the letter that stands for each number to discover five of the spelling words.

a	c	d	e	f	g	h	i	m	n	o	p	r	s	t	u	x	z
1	2	3	4	5	6	7	8	9	10	11	12	13	14	15	16	17	18

1. ___ ___ ___ ___ ___ ___ ___ ___
   10 11 10 14 4 10 14 4

2. ___ ___ ___ ___ ___ ___ ___ ___ ___ ___
   3 8 14 2 11 16 13 1 6 4

3. ___ ___ ___ ___ ___ ___ ___ ___ ___ ___
   10 11 10 5 8 2 15 8 11 10

4. ___ ___ ___ ___ ___ ___ ___ ___ ___ ___ ___
   2 8 15 8 18 4 10 14 7 8 12

5. ___ ___ ___ ___ ___ ___ ___ ___ ___ ___ ___
   10 11 10 4 17 8 14 15 4 10 15

Now make a code for the word *championship*.

___ ___ ___ ___ ___ ___ ___ ___ ___ ___ ___ ___

Spellamadoodle

Write each spelling word on the outline of the drawing. You may use the words more than once. For fun, decorate the drawing.

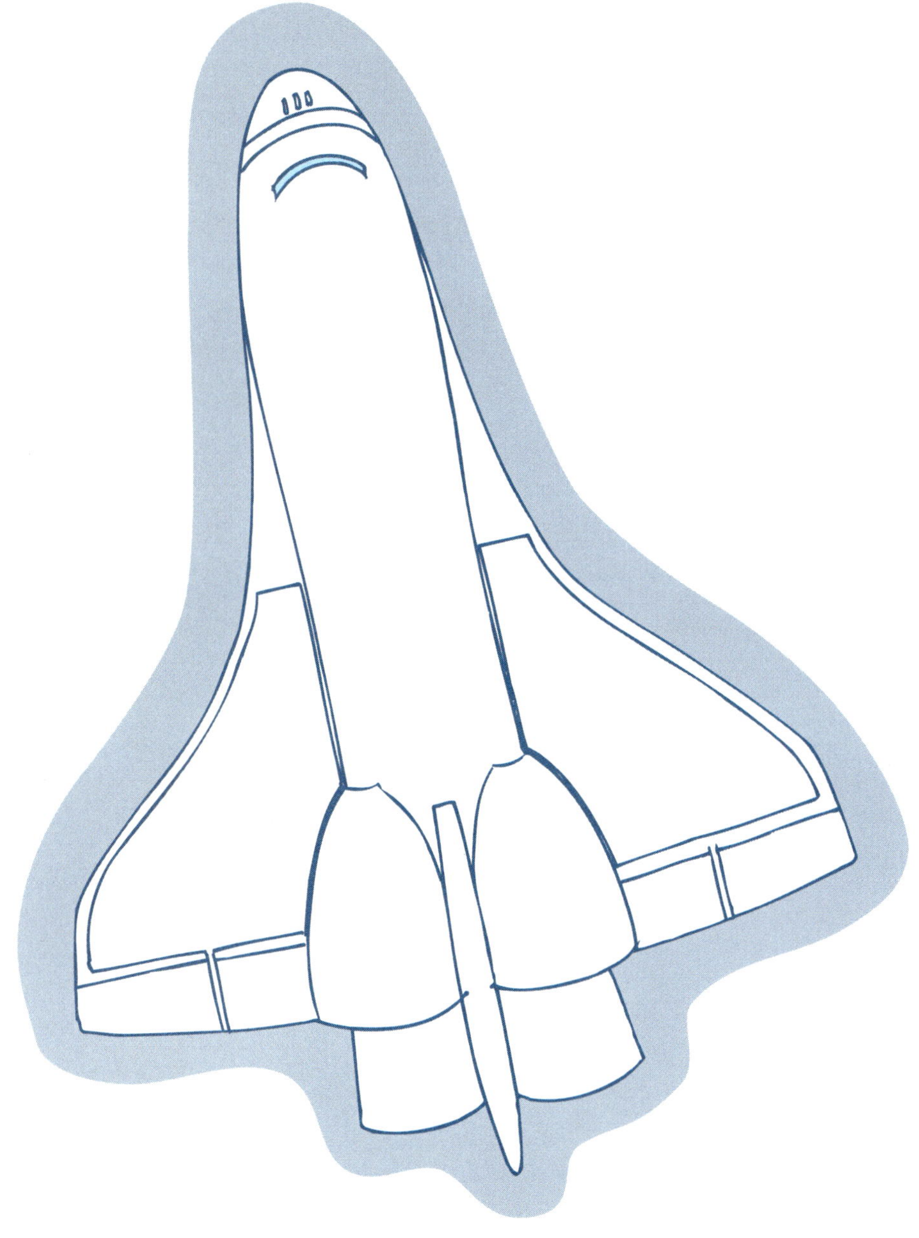

citizenship	partnership	ownership	championship
membership	dishonest	discourage	disagree
disgrace	nonsense	nonexistent	nonfiction

Skills:

Writing Spelling Words

Skills:

Performing an Experiment

Writing Experiment Results

Gravity Experiment

Perform the following gravity experiments and write your results below.

Experiment #1

Predict! What will happen if you drop two same-sized balls at the same time?

____

____

1. Gather a chair and two same-sized balls (or oranges or apples). Place newspapers around the chair.
2. Hold a ball in each hand. Extend your arms in front of you, holding the balls at the same height.
3. Let go of both balls at the same time. What happens?

____

____

Experiment #2

Predict! What will happen if you drop two different-sized balls at the same time?

____

____

1. Gather a large ball and a small ball (or fruit). Repeat the above experiment.
2. Hold a big ball in one hand and a small ball in the other. Extend your arms in front of you, holding the balls at the same height.
3. Let go of both balls at the same time. What happens?

____

____

Explain what you think are the reasons behind the results of both experiments.

____

____

____

A World Without Gravity

Skills:

Writing a Description

What would the Earth be like without gravity? What kinds of things would you be able to do? How would you eat? How would you sleep? What would school be like? Describe a world without gravity.

Edit Your Work

- I used complete sentences.
- I used correct spelling.
- I used correct capitalization and punctuation.

Microgravity

Find the correct answer. Fill in the circle.

1. Which sentence uses colons correctly?
   - ○ Please bake the following: cookies, cupcakes, and muffins.
   - ○ This clock says: that it's almost 1:30 p.m.
   - ○ You might disagree: but that is my opinion.

2. Which sentence is punctuated correctly?
   - ○ "The astronauts will be on TV at 500 p.m." Lisa told me."
   - ○ The astronauts will be on TV at 5:00 pm" Lisa told me
   - ○ "The astronauts will be on TV at 5:00 p.m.," Lisa told me.

3. Which of these defines the word *disgrace*?
   - ○ an argument
   - ○ opposite of honesty
   - ○ causing shame or disapproval

4. Which word is spelled correctly?
   - ○ nonexistant
   - ○ nonexistent
   - ○ nonexixtent

Spelling Test

Ask someone to test you on the spelling words.

1. ____________________
2. ____________________
3. ____________________
4. ____________________
5. ____________________
6. ____________________
7. ____________________
8. ____________________
9. ____________________
10. ____________________
11. ____________________
12. ____________________

5. Write the sentence correctly.

   she has a membirsip in a club that sends her only nunfichion books about champinship games

   ____

   ____

Meat-Eating Plants

Photo: dreamstime.com, Jack Schiffer

When you think of a predator, you probably don't picture a plant. You may want to rethink this! Most green plants make their own food. Carnivorous plants do, too, but they also need a reliable source of meat on the menu. These plants often grow in swampy soil where nitrogen and other nutrients are sparse. They get what they need by trapping and digesting insects and other small animals that have the misfortune of getting too close.

The Venus' flytrap grows in North and South Carolina. This deadly plant can attract a fly to its sweet nectar. Its hinged leaves, covered with tiny hairs and lined with bristles, are genuine traps. When the fly brushes against several hairs, the leaves snap closed. The bristles trap the fly inside, and the prey is digested within 10 days.

The pitcher plant of Southeast Asia is about three feet tall. Water and digestive juices collect inside its slippery "pitcher." Attracted to the abundant, sweet-smelling nectar, insects, frogs, and small rodents slide in and do not reappear.

Sundews are found around the world. The leaves are lined with miniature hairs tipped with sticky, sweet droplets. If an inquisitive insect gets trapped in a droplet, the leaf curls around the victim and digests it within five days.

Find It! Read the spelling words.
Check off the words you can find in the story.

☐ reappear	☐ rethink	☐ misspell	☐ misfortune
☐ misdirect	☐ zealous	☐ miniature	☐ inquisitive
☐ genuine	☐ reliable	☐ sparse	☐ abundant

How many spelling words did you find? _____

Skills:

Spelling Words with Prefixes **mis–** and **re–**

Spelling Theme Vocabulary

Visual Memory

Spelling Practice

Read and Spell	Copy and Spell	Spell It Again!
1. reappear		
2. rethink		
3. misspell		
4. misfortune		
5. misdirect		
6. zealous		
7. miniature		
8. inquisitive		
9. genuine		
10. reliable		
11. sparse		
12. abundant		

Word Study

Skills:

Spelling Words with Prefixes **mis–** and **re–**

Synonyms

Visual Memory

Fill in the missing prefixes to make spelling words.

re = again
mis = wrong, not

_______ spell (not spelling correctly)

_______ think (think again)

_______ direct (direct wrongly)

_______ fortune (not fortunate)

_______ appear (appear again)

Draw a line from each spelling word to its synonym.

abundant	• dependable
miniature	• real
zealous	• small
reliable	• questioning
inquisitive	• meager
sparse	• generous
genuine	• enthusiastic

Complete each sentence with a spelling word.

1. Lana knew the diamond was not fake; it was _______________ .
2. _______________ rainfall had caused many plants to dry up and die.
3. Sundews have _______________ hairs on their leaves.
4. _______________, sweet-smelling nectar attracts many insects.
5. You may want to _______________ your decision to buy that plant.

Skills:

Spelling Words with Prefixes **mis–** and **re–**

Spelling Theme Vocabulary

Visual Memory

Writing Complete Sentences

Spelling in Sentences

Circle the misspelled words in the sentences. Write them correctly on the lines.

1. Inqwisitive insects might want to rethinke what they eat.

   ______________________ ______________________

2. Abbundent hairs on the sundew help trap zelious insects.

   ______________________ ______________________

3. Try not to misppell the names of these gennuin plants.

   ______________________ ______________________

4. Sweet nectar might missdirict an insect to misfortine.

   ______________________ ______________________

5. Mineatur hairs on the plant may look sparce, but they're not.

   ______________________ ______________________

6. These relliuble flower buds will reapeare each year.

   ______________________ ______________________

Think of something that can be *abundant*. Write a sentence about it.

____

____

Think of something that is *genuine*. Write a sentence about it.

____

____

Working with Words

The pronouns **I**, **me**, **they**, and **them** follow specific usage rules.

- Use **I** and **they** in the subject.

I went alone. They picked me up.

- Use **me** and **them** in the predicate or after the preposition.

She went with me. I went with them.

Skills:

Using **I**, **me**, **they**, and **them**

Writing Complete Sentences

Circle the correct word to complete each sentence.

1. Krista and **I**/**me** are going to the greenhouse.
2. **They**/**Them** told us we could study the meat-eating plants.
3. **Me**/**I** will look at the famous sundew and Venus' flytrap.
4. Will you help **I**/**me** find these famous flowers?
5. Insects should be very cautious of **them**/**they**.
6. We finally found **them**/**they** in their own aisle.
7. **Them**/**They** look very hungry!
8. Perhaps you could show Krista and **me**/**I** how they eat.

Write a sentence using the word *I*.

____

____

Write a sentence using the word *me*.

____

____

Write a sentence using the word *they*.

____

____

Write a sentence using the word *them*.

____

____

Skills:

Context Clues

Writing Spelling Words

Watch Out!

Complete the paragraphs using words from the spelling list. You will use each word only once. One word won't be used.

reappear	rethink	misspell	misfortune
misdirect	zealous	miniature	inquisitive
genuine	reliable	sparse	abundant

Watch out, curious, ________________ little ant! You might get eaten by that hungry, ________________ plant! This may look like a good place to find food. The Venus' flytrap isn't a friendly plant at all, but a ________________ trap. You may want to ________________ having its sweet nectar for lunch. Many other insects before you have had the ________________ of falling into this trap. Don't let its sweetness ________________ you! Find your lunch somewhere else.

Hey, little ant! Watch out for those sundews, too. You may hardly be able to see those ________________ hairs. They may even seem thin and ________________. But there are enough little hairs to trap you. Believe me, I am a ________________ source. I've seen many an insect get tempted by these multitudes of ________________, sweet droplets. Once you go in, the leaf curls around you. You will never ________________. So, watch out!

Spellamadoodle

Skills:

Writing Spelling Words

Write each spelling word on the outline of the drawing. You may use the words more than once. For fun, decorate the drawing.

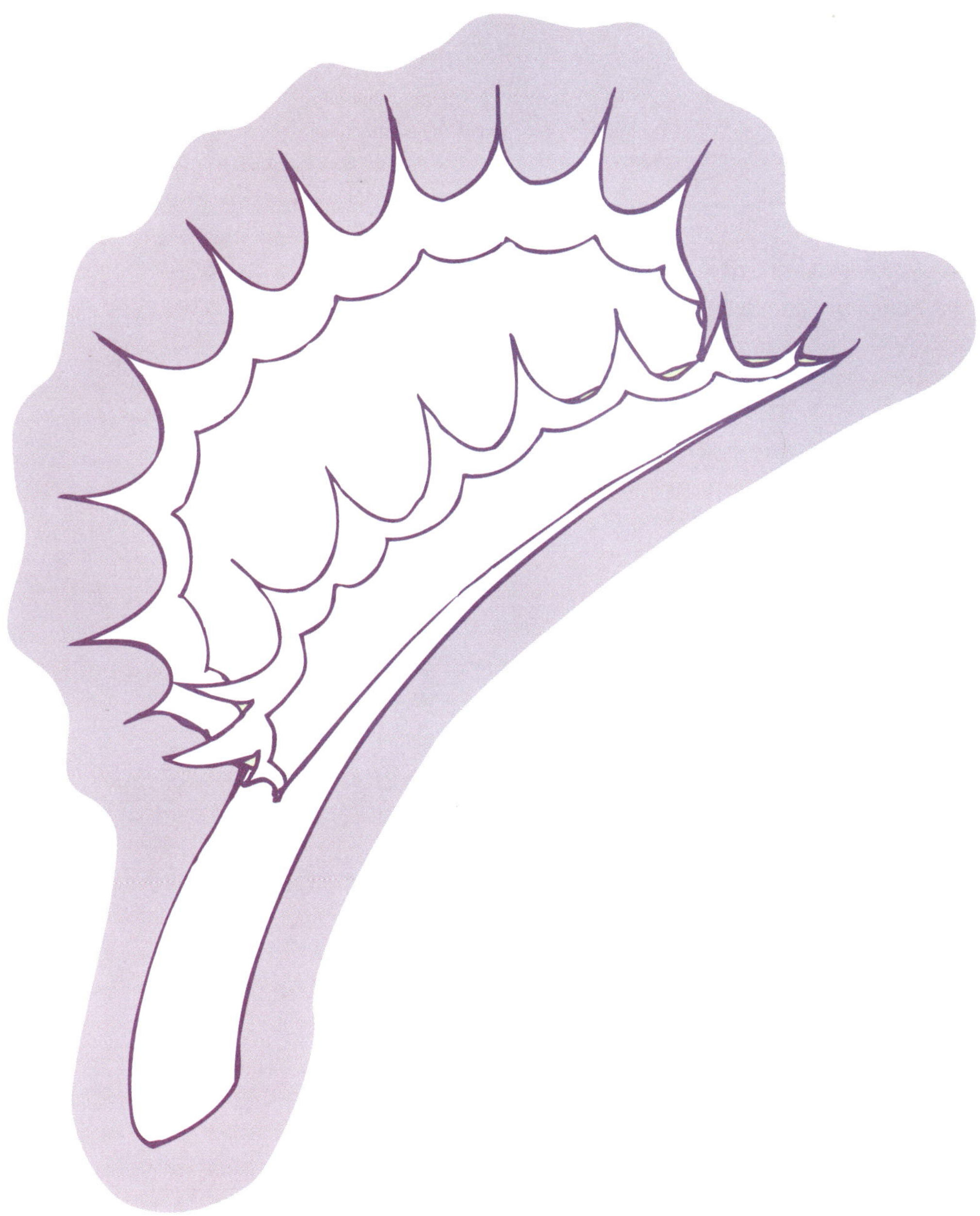

reappear	rethink	misspell	misfortune
misdirect	zealous	miniature	inquisitive
genuine	reliable	sparse	abundant

Skills:

Writing an Opinion

Eating Habits

Biology dictates which animals and plants are carnivores, herbivores, or omnivores. Humans, however, can make a choice as to their eating habits.

Which is your preference:

Being a carnivore (meat-eater)?

Being a herbivore (plant-eater)?

Being an omnivore (both a meat- and a plant-eater)?

Choose your preference and support your opinion. Give at least three reasons why you prefer to be a carnivore, a herbivore, or an omnivore.

Wild Plants

Skills:

Writing a Description

Now that you've read about these unusual meat-eating plants, make up your own wild plant! Instead of sticky hairs and sweet nectar, how does your plant trap food? What does your plant eat? What does it look like? What features does it have? Describe your wild plant below and then draw a picture of it.

Edit Your Work

- ◯ I used complete sentences.
- ◯ I used correct spelling.
- ◯ I used correct capitalization and punctuation.

Meat-Eating Plants

Find the correct answer. Fill in the circle.

1. Which sentence is written correctly?
   - ❍ Them look like nice plants to buy.
   - ❍ They are the plants we want to buy.
   - ❍ We gave the plants to they.

2. Which sentence is written correctly?
   - ❍ Tera and me own a pitcher plant.
   - ❍ Me and Tera own a pitcher plant.
   - ❍ That pitcher plant belongs to Tera and me.

3. Which word is a synonym for *zealous*?
   - ❍ generous
   - ❍ dependable
   - ❍ enthusiastic

4. Which word is spelled correctly?
   - ❍ inquisitive
   - ❍ inquisative
   - ❍ inquisiative

Spelling Test

Ask someone to test you on the spelling words.

1. ______________________
2. ______________________
3. ______________________
4. ______________________
5. ______________________
6. ______________________
7. ______________________
8. ______________________
9. ______________________
10. ______________________
11. ______________________
12. ______________________

5. Write the sentence correctly.

the inkwisative insect met its misfortoon in the sticky, mineatur hairs of the sundew

____

____

The Pony Express

WANTED!

Young, skinny, wiry fellows.
Must be expert riders.
Willing to risk death daily.
Orphans preferred.

This ad appeared in a newspaper over a century ago. A freight company was hiring young men to deliver mail on horseback across the country. From April 1860 to October 1861, the Pony Express delivered mail between St. Joseph, Missouri, and Sacramento, California.

About 180 riders took part. They didn't wear special uniforms. However, mail was carried in a unique saddlebag pouch called a "mochila." The riders were on the trail day and night, in any weather. The men rode for seven to ten hours a day and covered up to 100 miles. They stopped only for a fresh horse every ten to fifteen miles. The change did not interrupt the schedule. It must have been quite a spectacle. The rider would leap from the saddle of one tired horse into the saddle of a fresh one.

One-way delivery took about ten days in the summer and two weeks in the winter. The fastest delivery was seven days and seventeen hours. The completion of the coast-to-coast telegraph eventually bankrupted the Pony Express service. It ended in October 1861. During its short life, the Pony Express helped to unify the nation and earned the respect of the world.

Find It! Read the spelling words.
Check off the words you can find in the story.

- [ ] unify
- [ ] union
- [ ] unique
- [ ] century
- [ ] centennial
- [ ] interrupt
- [ ] bankrupt
- [ ] suspect
- [ ] respect
- [ ] spectacle
- [ ] uniform
- [ ] transform

How many spelling words did you find? _____

Skills:

Spelling Words with Prefixes **uni–** and **cent–**

Root Words **rupt**, **spec**, and **form**

Spelling Theme Vocabulary

Visual Memory

Spelling Practice

Read and Spell	Copy and Spell	Spell It Again!
1. unify		
2. union		
3. unique		
4. century		
5. centennial		
6. interrupt		
7. bankrupt		
8. suspect		
9. respect		
10. spectacle		
11. uniform		
12. transform		

Making Words

Fill in the missing letters to make spelling words.

___ ___ ___fy	bank ___ ___ ___t	trans ___ ___ ___m
___ ___ ___form	___ ___ ___tury	spect ___ ___ ___e
___ ___ ___on	re ___ ___ ___ct	un ___ ___ ___e
inter ___ ___ ___t	___ ___ ___pect	___ ___ ___tennial

Now, find and circle the spelling words in the word search. Words can go across, down, or diagonally.

W	A	I	N	T	E	R	R	U	P	T	E
U	R	M	O	U	R	E	S	P	E	C	T
T	N	C	Q	S	S	N	P	L	I	O	Y
S	U	I	E	E	B	O	C	K	U	W	A
O	N	U	O	N	I	A	M	E	N	B	S
U	I	C	E	N	T	E	N	N	I	A	L
L	F	A	L	C	S	U	R	T	F	N	A
A	Y	F	E	T	H	W	R	S	O	K	U
R	E	P	J	K	A	D	E	Y	R	R	T
P	S	U	S	P	E	C	T	N	M	U	R
S	A	C	O	L	P	A	E	Y	I	P	E
T	R	A	N	S	F	O	R	M	U	T	S

Skills:

Spelling Words with Prefixes **uni–** and **cent–**

Root Words **rupt**, **spec**, and **form**

Spelling Theme Vocabulary

Visual Memory

Visual Discrimination

Skills:

Spelling Words with Prefixes **uni–** and **cent–**

Root Words **rupt**, **spec**, and **form**

Spelling Theme Vocabulary

Visual Memory

Spelling in Context

Spell Check

Circle the word in each row that is spelled correctly.

1. unicke	unique	uneque
2. spekticle	spectikl	spectacle
3. century	sentery	cenchure
4. uniform	uniformme	unniform
5. intterupt	interrupt	inturrupt
6. sentenial	centeneal	centennial
7. suscpect	suspect	susspict
8. unify	unnify	uniffey
9. respect	respict	risppect
10. unean	unnion	union
11. bancrupt	bankrupt	benckrupt
12. transforme	transform	trannsfirm

Circle the misspelled words in the sentences. Write them correctly on the lines.

1. The Pony Express earned reespekt as it helped unnufy a nation.

____

____

2. This unicque mail system would trannsforme the communication industry.

____

____

Pronoun Replacements

Skills:

Identifying Pronouns and Their Antecedents

The antecedent of a pronoun is the noun or nouns to which the pronoun refers. The antecedent doesn't have to be in the same sentence as the pronoun.

The rider rode to a station where a fresh horse was waiting for him.
(antecedent) (pronoun)

Circle each pronoun. Then draw an arrow from the pronoun to its antecedent.

1. The Pony Express helped unify a nation. It was very successful.
2. About 180 riders took part. They were on the trail day and night.
3. Riders traveled in any weather, and they never stopped.
4. Delivery took 10 days in the summer, and it took two weeks in the winter.
5. Many people depended on the Pony Express, and they were thankful.
6. A rider must be an expert rider, and he must be willing to risk death.
7. The mochila was a saddlebag pouch. It contained mail.
8. The horses were fast, but they did tire after long hours of running.

Skills:

Matching Words with Their Meanings

Make a Match

Write the letter of the definition that matches each spelling word.

______ 1. bankrupt		a. an unusual sight or display
______ 2. centennial		b. to make a great change in something
______ 3. century		c. to unite
______ 4. interrupt		d. a 100th anniversary
______ 5. respect		e. to stop by breaking in on
______ 6. spectacle		f. the joining together of two or more things or people to form a larger group
______ 7. suspect		g. being the only one of its kind
______ 8. transform		h. unable to pay one's debts
______ 9. uniform		i. to think of as guilty without proof
______ 10. unify		j. admiration or high regard
______ 11. union		k. a period of one hundred years
______ 12. unique		l. a special set of clothes worn by members of a group or organization

Spellamadoodle

Write each spelling word on the outline of the drawing. You may use the words more than once. For fun, decorate the drawing.

unify	union	unique	century
centennial	interrupt	bankrupt	suspect
respect	spectacle	uniform	transform

Skills:

Writing Spelling Words

Skills:

Writing an Advertisement

Wanted! Pony Express Riders

Use the information from the story to write your own advertisement for the Pony Express. Think about the qualities one should have to ride for the Express. Refer back to information from the newspaper ad on page 113. List the qualities, skills, and characteristics for the perfect rider.

WANTED!

On the Trail

Skills:

Writing a Creative Story

You are a Pony Express rider. Write about a day in your life on the trail. Where are you going? What kind of mail are you carrying? Who do you meet along the way? What kind of difficulties do you face? Write about it below.

Edit Your Work

- ○ I used complete sentences.
- ○ I used correct spelling.
- ○ I used correct capitalization and punctuation.

The Pony Express

Find the correct answer. Fill in the circle.

1. In which sentence are the pronoun and its antecedent underlined?
   - ○ When Ted joined the Express, he became one of its best riders.
   - ○ When Ted joined the Express, he became one of its best riders.
   - ○ When Ted joined the Express, he became one of its best riders.

2. In which sentence are the pronoun and its antecedent underlined?
   - ○ Mrs. Waters was worried as she kissed her son good-bye.
   - ○ Mrs. Waters was worried as she kissed her son good-bye.
   - ○ Mrs. Waters was worried as she kissed her son good-bye.

3. Which of these defines the word *unify*?
   - ○ to think as quilty
   - ○ to stop by breaking in on
   - ○ to join together into a whole or a unit

4. Which word is spelled correctly?
   - ○ interupt
   - ○ interrupt
   - ○ interruppt

Spelling Test

Ask someone to test you on the spelling words.

1. ______________________
2. ______________________
3. ______________________
4. ______________________
5. ______________________
6. ______________________
7. ______________________
8. ______________________
9. ______________________
10. ______________________
11. ______________________
12. ______________________

5. Write the sentence correctly.

i suspict that this rider is a uneque man whose skills earn him much respeck

____

____

Test Your Skill—Record Form

Unit	Test Page	Topic	Test Your Skills Score (5 possible)	Spelling Test Score (12 possible)
1	12	Tall Tale Heroes		
2	22	At Your Fingertips		
3	32	Elizabeth Blackwell		
4	42	The Duckbilled Platypus		
5	52	The Grand Canyon		
6	62	Amazing Morse		
7	72	Race of Mercy		
8	82	The Olympic Flame		
9	92	Inuit Snowhouses		
10	102	Microgravity		
11	112	Meat-Eating Plants		
12	122	The Pony Express		

Pull-out Spelling Lists

Use these lists to give spelling tests, post on the refrigerator, and for extra practice.

Unit 1 Tall Tale Heroes	Unit 2 At Your Fingertips	Unit 3 Elizabeth Blackwell
1. tedious	1. although	1. anywhere
2. straight	2. envelope	2. occasion
3. eagerly	3. often	3. everybody
4. famous	4. officer	4. old-fashioned
5. pleasant	5. describe	5. meanwhile
6. frequent	6. scientific	6. footsteps
7. acre	7. distinct	7. opportunity
8. anticipate	8. utilize	8. outstanding
9. achievement	9. valuable	9. recommend
10. persuade	10. thumbprint	10. studied
11. campaign	11. fugitive	11. opposite
12. freighter	12. customary	12. knowledge

Pull-out Spelling Lists

Use these lists to give spelling tests, post on the refrigerator, and for extra practice.

Unit 4 The Duckbilled Platypus	Unit 5 The Grand Canyon	Unit 6 Amazing Morse
1. creature	1. opinion	1. persistent
2. feature	2. appearance	2. equivalent
3. puncture	3. national	3. brilliant
4. leisure	4. argument	4. significant
5. pleasure	5. shortage	5. attendant
6. natural	6. ordinary	6. impatient
7. enough	7. succession	7. ambitious
8. physical	8. observation	8. ocean
9. efficient	9. estimation	9. establish
10. flexible	10. action	10. surely
11. oily	11. persuasion	11. conversation
12. turmoil	12. expression	12. official

Pull-out Spelling Lists

Use these lists to give spelling tests, post on the refrigerator, and for extra practice.

Unit 7 Race of Mercy	Unit 8 The Olympic Flame	Unit 9 Inuit Snowhouses
1. lovable	1. independent	1. geography
2. sensible	2. inconvenient	2. geology
3. vicious	3. immortal	3. geologist
4. precious	4. immediate	4. permanently
5. amazement	5. underneath	5. especially
6. successful	6. underestimate	6. immediately
7. doubtful	7. uncertain	7. temporarily
8. powerless	8. unreliable	8. perfectly
9. tireless	9. enact	9. sincerely
10. curious	10. react	10. lengthen
11. numerous	11. transport	11. strengthen
12. grateful	12. portable	12. frighten

Pull-out Spelling Lists

Use these lists to give spelling tests, post on the refrigerator, and for extra practice.

Unit 10 Microgravity	Unit 11 Meat-Eating Plants	Unit 12 The Pony Express
1. citizenship	1. reappear	1. unify
2. partnership	2. rethink	2. union
3. ownership	3. misspell	3. unique
4. championship	4. misfortune	4. century
5. membership	5. misdirect	5. centennial
6. dishonest	6. zealous	6. interrupt
7. discourage	7. miniature	7. bankrupt
8. disagree	8. inquisitive	8. suspect
9. disgrace	9. genuine	9. respect
10. nonsense	10. reliable	10. spectacle
11. nonexistent	11. sparse	11. uniform
12. nonfiction	12. abundant	12. transform

Answer Key

Page 3

Tall Tale Heroes

Life for American pioneers was hard, and their work was often tedious. For entertainment, they told funny stories called "tall tales." The stories had larger-than-life characters and were filled with exaggerations. Two famous tall tale characters are Paul Bunyan and Pecos Bill.

Imagine a giant lumberjack who could topple an acre of trees with one hand. That was Paul Bunyan. Bunyan was so big that he had to eat 40 bowls of porridge just to whet his appetite. His faithful companion was an immense blue ox named Babe. Their rain-filled footprints became the 10,000 lakes of Minnesota. According to stories, surviving in the North Woods was also an achievement. One winter, it was so cold that Babe's milk turned straight to ice cream!

Do you know of any cowboy who would ride a horse named Widow Maker? That was Pecos Bill, who also galloped around on a mountain lion. Legend says that Bill fell from his parents' wagon when he was a baby. Coyotes rescued Bill and raised him in the wild. He could rope a whole herd of cattle at once, or even lasso a cyclone. And when he anticipated trouble, he carried a live rattlesnake as a whip. Bill's girlfriend was also famous for her frequent stunts. Slue-Foot Sue once took a pleasant ride on a giant catfish down the Rio Grande!

Find It! Read the spelling words. Check off the words you can find in the story.

- ✓ tedious
- ✓ pleasant
- ✓ achievement
- ✓ straight
- ✓ frequent
- ☐ persuade
- ☐ eagerly
- ✓ acre
- ☐ campaign
- ✓ famous
- ✓ anticipate
- ☐ freighter

How many spelling words did you find? 8

©2005 by Evan-Moor Corp. • EMC 4542 • Spell & Write UNIT 1 3

Page 5

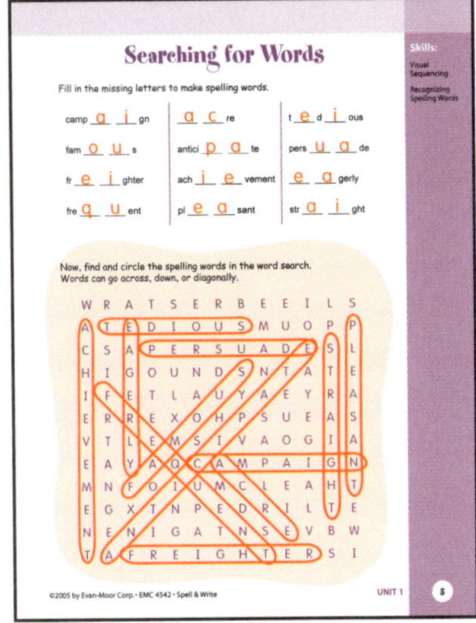

Searching for Words

Skills: Visual Sequencing; Recognizing Spelling Words

Fill in the missing letters to make spelling words.

camp a i gn	a c re	t e d i ous
fam o u s	antici p a te	pers u a de
fr e i ghter	ach i e vement	e a gerly
fre q u ent	pl e a sant	str a i ght

Now, find and circle the spelling words in the word search. Words can go across, down, or diagonally.

```
W R A T S E R B E E I L S
A T E D I O U S M U O P P
C S A P E R S U A D E S L
H I G O U N D S N T A T E
I F E T L A U Y A E Y R A
E R R E X O H P S U E A S
V T L E M S I V A O G I A
E A Y A Q C A M P A I G N
M N F O I U M C L E A H T
E G X T N P E D R I L T E
N E N I G A T N S E V B W
T A F R E I G H T E R S I
```

©2005 by Evan-Moor Corp. • EMC 4542 • Spell & Write UNIT 1 5

Page 6

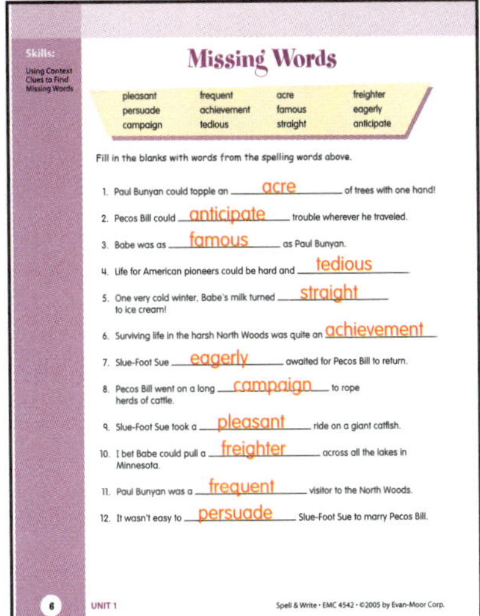

Missing Words

Skills: Using Context Clues to Find Missing Words

pleasant, persuade, campaign, frequent, achievement, tedious, acre, famous, straight, freighter, eagerly, anticipate

Fill in the blanks with words from the spelling words above.

1. Paul Bunyan could topple an acre of trees with one hand!
2. Pecos Bill could anticipate trouble wherever he traveled.
3. Babe was as famous as Paul Bunyan.
4. Life for American pioneers could be hard and tedious.
5. One very cold winter, Babe's milk turned straight to ice cream!
6. Surviving life in the harsh North Woods was quite an achievement.
7. Slue-Foot Sue eagerly awaited for Pecos Bill to return.
8. Pecos Bill went on a long campaign to rope herds of cattle.
9. Slue-Foot Sue took a pleasant ride on a giant catfish.
10. I bet Babe could pull a freighter across all the lakes in Minnesota.
11. Paul Bunyan was a frequent visitor to the North Woods.
12. It wasn't easy to persuade Slue-Foot Sue to marry Pecos Bill.

6 UNIT 1 Spell & Write • EMC 4542 • ©2005 by Evan-Moor Corp.

Page 7

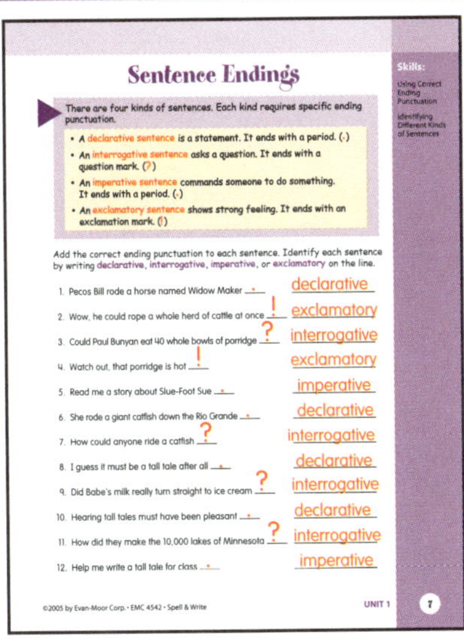

Sentence Endings

Skills: Using Correct Ending Punctuation; Identifying Different Kinds of Sentences

There are four kinds of sentences. Each kind requires specific ending punctuation.

- A declarative sentence is a statement. It ends with a period. (.)
- An interrogative sentence asks a question. It ends with a question mark. (?)
- An imperative sentence commands someone to do something. It ends with a period. (.)
- An exclamatory sentence shows strong feeling. It ends with an exclamation mark. (!)

Add the correct ending punctuation to each sentence. Identify each sentence by writing declarative, interrogative, imperative, or exclamatory on the line.

1. Pecos Bill rode a horse named Widow Maker . declarative
2. Wow, he could rope a whole herd of cattle at once ! exclamatory
3. Could Paul Bunyan eat 40 whole bowls of porridge ? interrogative
4. Watch out, that porridge is hot ! exclamatory
5. Read me a story about Slue-Foot Sue . imperative
6. She rode a giant catfish down the Rio Grande . declarative
7. How could anyone ride a catfish ? interrogative
8. I guess it must be a tall tale after all . declarative
9. Did Babe's milk really turn straight to ice cream ? interrogative
10. Hearing tall tales must have been pleasant . declarative
11. How did they make the 10,000 lakes of Minnesota ? interrogative
12. Help me write a tall tale for class . imperative

©2005 by Evan-Moor Corp. • EMC 4542 • Spell & Write UNIT 1 7

Page 8

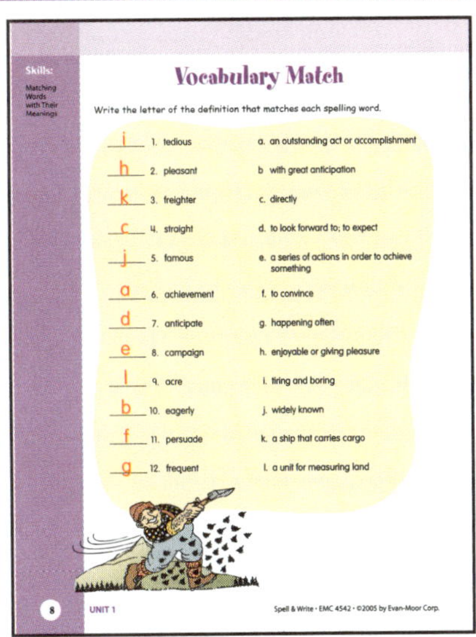

Vocabulary Match

Skills: Matching Words with Their Meanings

Write the letter of the definition that matches each spelling word.

Answer	Word	Definition
i	1. tedious	a. an outstanding act or accomplishment
h	2. pleasant	b. with great anticipation
k	3. freighter	c. directly
c	4. straight	d. to look forward to; to expect
j	5. famous	e. a series of actions in order to achieve something
a	6. achievement	f. to convince
d	7. anticipate	g. happening often
e	8. campaign	h. enjoyable or giving pleasure
l	9. acre	i. tiring and boring
b	10. eagerly	j. widely known
f	11. persuade	k. a ship that carries cargo
g	12. frequent	l. a unit for measuring land

8 UNIT 1 Spell & Write • EMC 4542 • ©2005 by Evan-Moor Corp.

Page 10

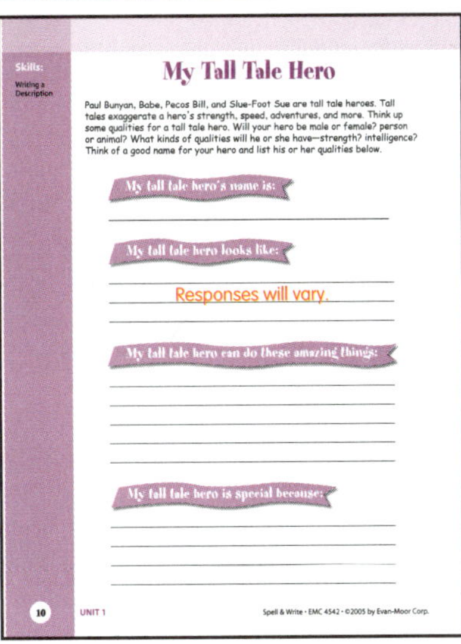

My Tall Tale Hero

Skills: Writing a Description

Paul Bunyan, Babe, Pecos Bill, and Slue-Foot Sue are tall tale heroes. Tall tales exaggerate a hero's strength, speed, adventures, and more. Think up some qualities for a tall tale hero. Will your hero be male or female? person or animal? What kinds of qualities will he or she have—strength? intelligence? Think of a good name for your hero and list his or her qualities below.

My tall tale hero's name is:

My tall tale hero looks like:

Responses will vary.

My tall tale hero can do these amazing things:

My tall tale hero is special because:

10 UNIT 1 Spell & Write • EMC 4542 • ©2005 by Evan-Moor Corp.

Page 11

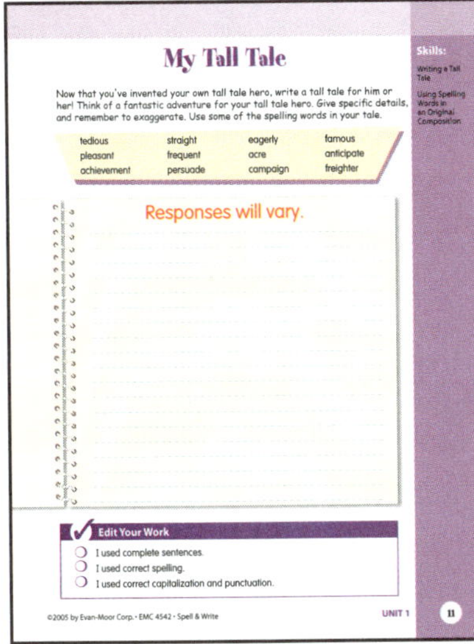

My Tall Tale

Skills: Writing a Tall Tale; Using Spelling Words in an Original Composition

Now that you've invented your own tall tale hero, write a tall tale for him or her! Think of a fantastic adventure for your tall tale hero. Give specific details, and remember to exaggerate. Use some of the spelling words in your tale.

tedious, pleasant, achievement, straight, frequent, persuade, eagerly, acre, campaign, famous, anticipate, freighter

Responses will vary.

Edit Your Work

- ❍ I used complete sentences.
- ❍ I used correct spelling.
- ❍ I used correct capitalization and punctuation.

©2005 by Evan-Moor Corp. • EMC 4542 • Spell & Write UNIT 1 11

Page 12

Test Your Skills: Tall Tale Heroes

Find the correct answer. Fill in the circle.

1. Which of the following is an interrogative sentence?
   - ❍ Legends and tall tales are similar kinds of stories.
   - ● Have you ever written a tall tale?
   - ❍ Babe's milk got so cold it turned to ice cream!
2. Which of the following is an imperative sentence?
   - ❍ Coyotes raised Pecos Bill in the wild.
   - ❍ Pecos Bill carried a rattlesnake as a whip!
   - ● Read me a story about Paul Bunyan and Babe.
3. Which of these is a definition for the word *tedious*?
   - ❍ enjoyable
   - ● tired and boring
   - ❍ widely known
4. Which word is spelled correctly?
   - ● achievement
   - ❍ achevement
   - ❍ acheivement

Spelling Test

Ask someone to test you on the spelling words.

1. ___
2. ___
3. ___
4. ___
5. ___
6. ___
7. ___
8. ___
9. ___
10. ___
11. ___
12. ___

5. Write the sentence correctly.

the faimus hero eegerley cut down an acer of trees—an amazing acheivment

The famous hero eagerly cut down an acre of trees—an amazing achievement.

12 ASSESSMENT 1 Spell & Write • EMC 4542 • ©2005 by Evan-Moor Corp.

Page 13

At Your Fingertips

Twins often have the same hair and eye color. But they don't have the same fingerprints or thumbprints. No two people have prints that are exactly alike. Fingerprints have distinct ridges, spirals, loops, splits, and dots. Although prints expand as a person grows, they don't change. Only deep injuries or disease can sometimes alter them.

In 1686, Professor Marcello Malpighi was the first to fully describe ridges, spirals, and loops in fingerprints. His descriptions are still used today. Sir Francis Galton, a British scientist, noted that fingerprints could be valuable to identify people. He said that the odds of two sets of fingerprints being the same were one in 64 billion! In 1892, he published a book entitled *Fingerprints*. It included the first scientific classification system. That year, a police officer in Argentina captured a fugitive who was wanted for murder. He was able to utilize a bloody fingerprint to prove her guilt. Fingerprints had become an important tool for the police and the courts.

In 1924, the United States Congress created the Identification Division of the F.B.I. Its files hold more than 40 million fingerprint records!

Find It! Read the spelling words. Check off the words you can find in the story.

✓ although	envelope	✓ often	✓ officer
✓ describe	✓ scientific	✓ distinct	✓ utilize
✓ valuable	✓ thumbprint	✓ fugitive	customary

How many spelling words did you find? 10

©2005 by Evan-Moor Corp. • EMC 4542 • Spell & Write UNIT 2 13

Page 15

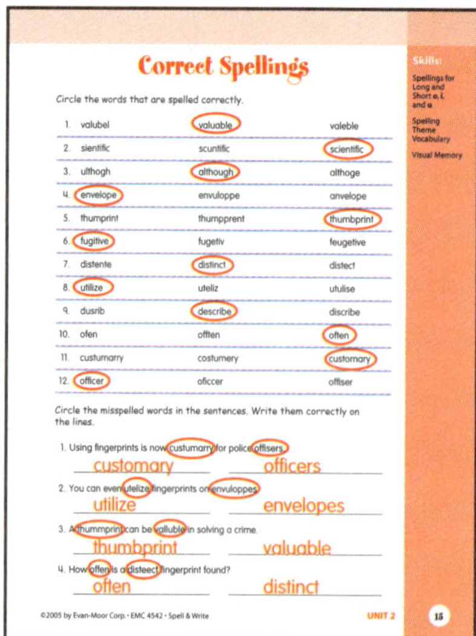

Correct Spellings

Skills: Spellings for Long and Short a, i, and u; Spelling Theme Vocabulary; Visual Memory

Circle the words that are spelled correctly.

1.	volubel	(valuable)	valeble
2.	sientific	scuntific	(scientific)
3.	ulthogh	(although)	althoge
4.	(envelope)	envuloppe	anvelope
5.	thumprint	thumpprent	(thumbprint)
6.	(fugitive)	fugetiv	feugetive
7.	distente	(distinct)	distect
8.	(utilize)	uteliz	utilise
9.	dusrib	(describe)	discribe
10.	ofen	offen	(often)
11.	custumary	costumery	(customary)
12.	(officer)	oficcer	offiser

Circle the misspelled words in the sentences. Write them correctly on the lines.

1. Using fingerprints is now (custumary) for police (offisers).
customary officers
2. You can even (utelize) fingerprints on (envuloppes).
utilize envelopes
3. A (thummprint) can be (valluble) in solving a crime.
thumbprint valuable
4. How (offen) is a (disteect) fingerprint found?
often distinct

©2005 by Evan-Moor Corp. • EMC 4542 • Spell & Write UNIT 2 15

Page 16

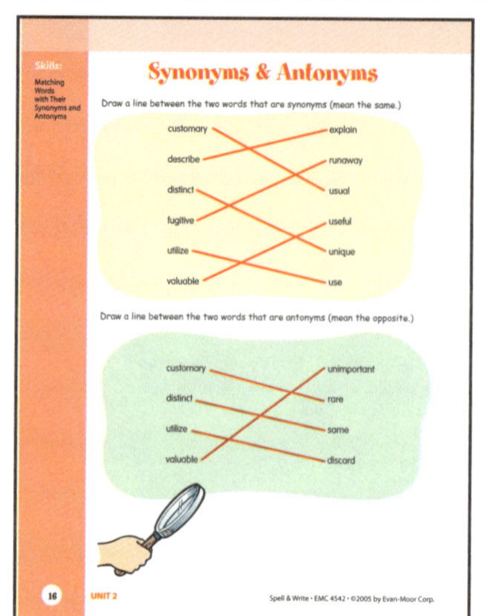

Synonyms & Antonyms

Skills: Matching Words with Their Synonyms and Antonyms

Draw a line between the two words that are synonyms (mean the same.)

customary — usual
describe — explain
distinct — unique
fugitive — runaway
utilize — use
valuable — useful

Draw a line between the two words that are antonyms (mean the opposite.)

customary — rare
distinct — same
utilize — discard
valuable — unimportant

16 UNIT 2 Spell & Write • EMC 4542 • ©2005 by Evan-Moor Corp.

Page 17

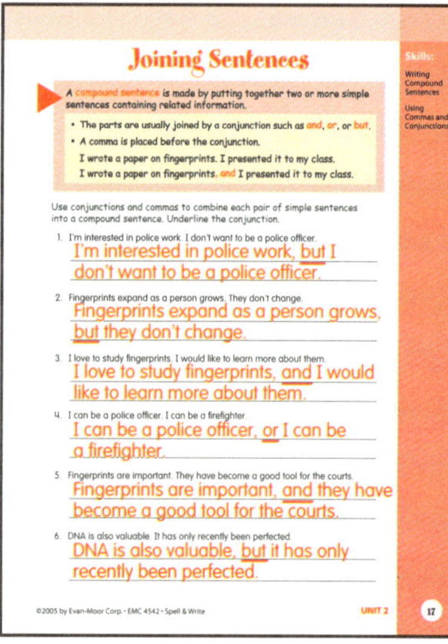

Joining Sentences

Skills: Writing Compound Sentences; Using Commas and Conjunctions

A compound sentence is made by putting together two or more simple sentences containing related information.

- The parts are usually joined by a conjunction such as *and*, *or*, or *but*.
- A comma is placed before the conjunction.

I wrote a paper on fingerprints. I presented it to my class.
I wrote a paper on fingerprints, and I presented it to my class.

Use conjunctions and commas to combine each pair of simple sentences into a compound sentence. Underline the conjunction.

1. I'm interested in police work. I don't want to be a police officer.
I'm interested in police work, but I don't want to be a police officer.
2. Fingerprints expand as a person grows. They don't change.
Fingerprints expand as a person grows, but they don't change.
3. I love to study fingerprints. I would like to learn more about them.
I love to study fingerprints, and I would like to learn more about them.
4. I can be a police officer. I can be a firefighter.
I can be a police officer, or I can be a firefighter.
5. Fingerprints are important. They have become a good tool for the courts.
Fingerprints are important, and they have become a good tool for the courts.
6. DNA is also valuable. It has only recently been perfected.
DNA is also valuable, but it has only recently been perfected.

©2005 by Evan-Moor Corp. • EMC 4542 • Spell & Write UNIT 2 17

Page 18

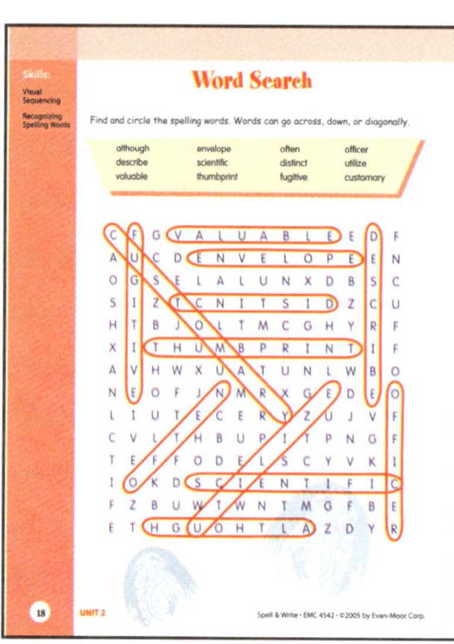

Word Search

Skills: Visual Sequencing; Recognizing Spelling Words

Find and circle the spelling words. Words can go across, down, or diagonally.

although	envelope	often	officer
describe	scientific	distinct	utilize
valuable	thumbprint	fugitive	customary

C F G V A L U A B L E E D F
A U C D E N V E L O P E E N
O G S E L A L U N X D B S C
S I Z T C N I T S I D Z C U
H T B J O L T M C G H Y R F
X I T H U M B P R I N T I F
A V H W X U A T U N L W B O
N E O F J N M R X G E D E O
L I U T E C E R Y Z U J V F
C V L T H B U P I T P N G F
T E F F O D E L S C Y V K I
I O K D S C I E N T I F I C
F Z B U W T W N T M G F B E
E T H G U O H T L A Z D Y R

18 UNIT 2 Spell & Write • EMC 4542 • ©2005 by Evan-Moor Corp.

Page 20

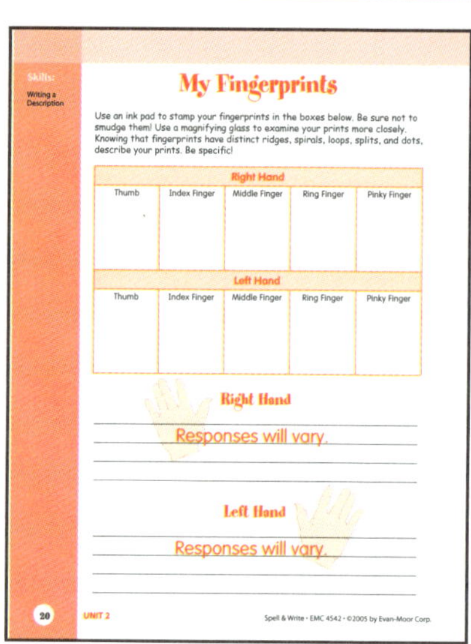

My Fingerprints

Skills: Writing a Description

Use an ink pad to stamp your fingerprints in the boxes below. Be sure not to smudge them! Use a magnifying glass to examine your prints more closely. Knowing that fingerprints have distinct ridges, spirals, loops, splits, and dots, describe your prints. Be specific!

Right Hand				
Thumb	Index Finger	Middle Finger	Ring Finger	Pinky Finger
Left Hand				
Thumb	Index Finger	Middle Finger	Ring Finger	Pinky Finger

Right Hand

Responses will vary.

Left Hand

Responses will vary.

20 UNIT 2 Spell & Write • EMC 4542 • ©2005 by Evan-Moor Corp.

Page 21

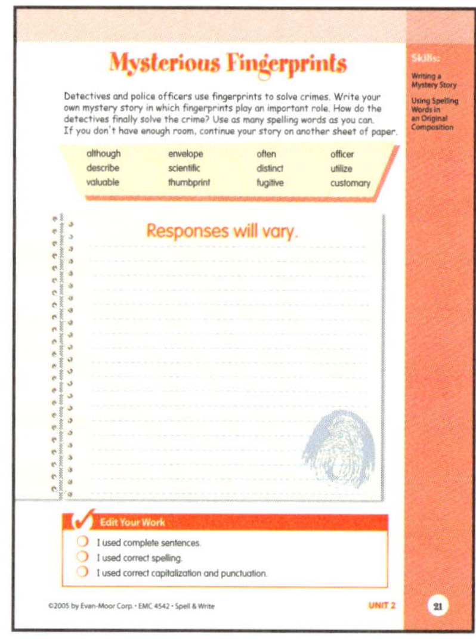

Mysterious Fingerprints

Skills: Writing a Mystery Story; Using Spelling Words in an Original Composition

Detectives and police officers use fingerprints to solve crimes. Write your own mystery story in which fingerprints play an important role. How do the detectives finally solve the crime? Use as many spelling words as you can. If you don't have enough room, continue your story on another sheet of paper.

although	envelope	often	officer
describe	scientific	distinct	utilize
valuable	thumbprint	fugitive	customary

Responses will vary.

Edit Your Work

- I used complete sentences.
- I used correct spelling.
- I used correct capitalization and punctuation.

©2005 by Evan-Moor Corp. • EMC 4542 • Spell & Write UNIT 2 21

Page 22

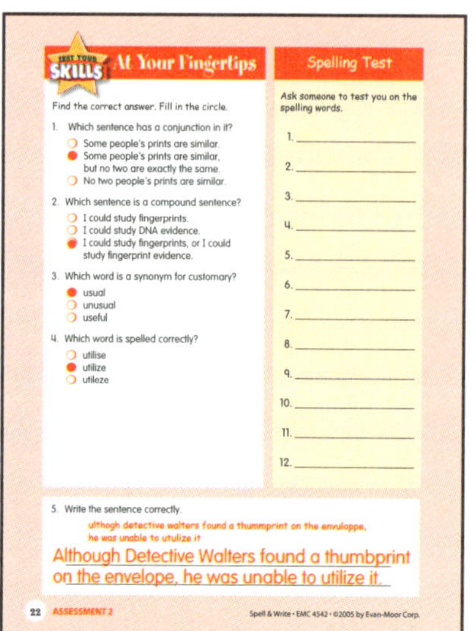

Test Your Skills: At Your Fingertips

Find the correct answer. Fill in the circle.

1. Which sentence has a conjunction in it?
   - Some people's prints are similar.
   - ● Some people's prints are similar, but no two are exactly the same.
   - No two people's prints are similar.
2. Which sentence is a compound sentence?
   - I could study fingerprints.
   - I could study DNA evidence.
   - ● I could study fingerprints, or I could study fingerprint evidence.
3. Which word is a synonym for customary?
   - ● usual
   - unusual
   - useful
4. Which word is spelled correctly?
   - utilise
   - ● utilize
   - utileze

Spelling Test

Ask someone to test you on the spelling words.

1. ___
2. ___
3. ___
4. ___
5. ___
6. ___
7. ___
8. ___
9. ___
10. ___
11. ___
12. ___

5. Write the sentence correctly.

ulthogh detective walters found a thummprint on the envuloppe, he was unable to utulize it

Although Detective Walters found a thumbprint on the envelope, he was unable to utilize it.

22 ASSESSMENT 2 Spell & Write • EMC 4542 • ©2005 by Evan-Moor Corp.

Page 23

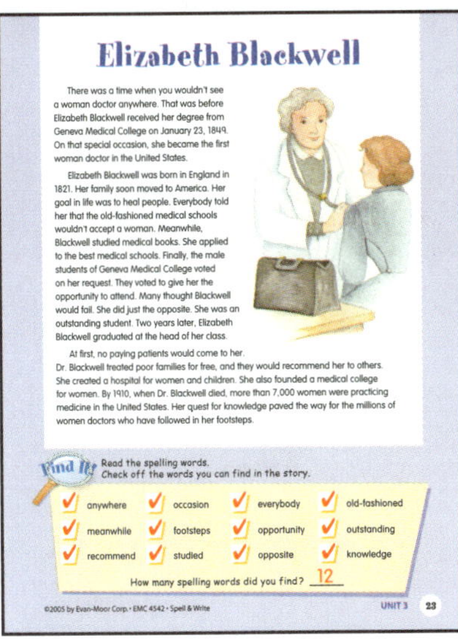

Elizabeth Blackwell

There was a time when you wouldn't see a woman doctor anywhere. That was before Elizabeth Blackwell received her degree from Geneva Medical College on January 23, 1849. On that special occasion, she became the first woman doctor in the United States.

Elizabeth Blackwell was born in England in 1821. Her family soon moved to America. Her goal in life was to heal people. Everybody told her that the old-fashioned medical schools wouldn't accept a woman. Meanwhile, Blackwell studied medical books. She applied to the best medical schools. Finally, the male students of Geneva Medical College voted on her request. They voted to give her the opportunity to attend. Many thought Blackwell would fail. She did just the opposite. She was an outstanding student. Two years later, Elizabeth Blackwell graduated at the head of her class.

At first, no paying patients would come to her. Dr. Blackwell treated poor families for free, and they would recommend her to others. She created a hospital for women and children. She also founded a medical college for women. By 1910, when Dr. Blackwell died, more than 7,000 women were practicing medicine in the United States. Her quest for knowledge paved the way for the millions of women doctors who have followed in her footsteps.

Find It! Read the spelling words. Check off the words you can find in the story.

✓ anywhere ✓ occasion ✓ everybody ✓ old-fashioned
✓ meanwhile ✓ footsteps ✓ opportunity ✓ outstanding
✓ recommend ✓ studied ✓ opposite ✓ knowledge

How many spelling words did you find? 12

©2005 by Evan-Moor Corp. • EMC 4542 • Spell & Write UNIT 3 23

Page 25

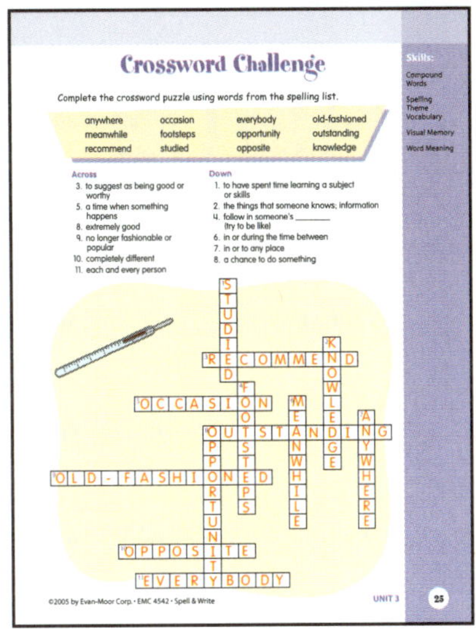

Crossword Challenge

Complete the crossword puzzle using words from the spelling list.

anywhere occasion everybody old-fashioned
meanwhile footsteps opportunity outstanding
recommend studied opposite knowledge

Across
3. to suggest as being good or worthy
5. a time when something happens
8. extremely good
9. no longer fashionable or popular
10. completely different
11. each and every person

Down
1. to have spent time learning a subject or skills
2. the things that someone knows; information
4. follow in someone's ______ (try to be like)
6. in or during the time between
7. in or to any place
8. a chance to do something

©2005 by Evan-Moor Corp. • EMC 4542 • Spell & Write UNIT 3 25

Skills: Compound Words; Spelling Theme Vocabulary; Visual Memory; Word Meaning

Page 26

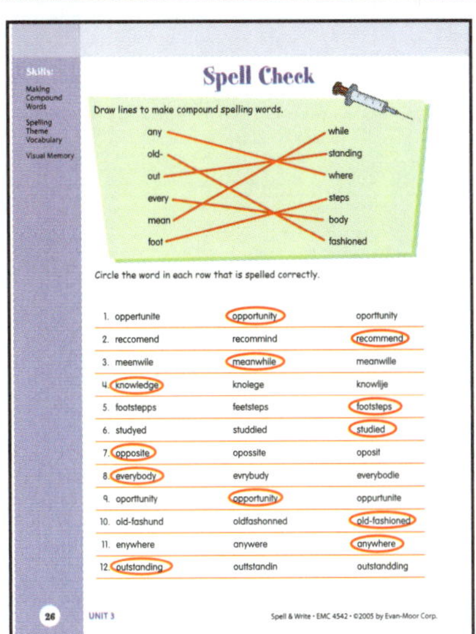

Spell Check

Skills: Making Compound Words; Spelling Theme Vocabulary; Visual Memory

Draw lines to make compound spelling words.

any	while
old-	standing
out	where
every	steps
mean	body
foot	fashioned

Circle the word in each row that is spelled correctly.

1.	oppertunite	(opportunity)	oportunity
2.	reccomend	recommind	(recommend)
3.	meenwile	(meanwhile)	meanwille
4.	(knowledge)	knolege	knowlije
5.	footstepps	feetsteps	(footsteps)
6.	studyed	studdied	(studied)
7.	(opposite)	opossite	oposit
8.	(everybody)	evrybudy	everybodie
9.	oportunity	(opportunity)	oppurtunite
10.	old-fashund	oldfashonned	(old-fashioned)
11.	enywhere	anywere	(anywhere)
12.	(outstanding)	outtstandin	outstandding

26 UNIT 3 Spell & Write • EMC 4542 • ©2005 by Evan-Moor Corp.

Page 27

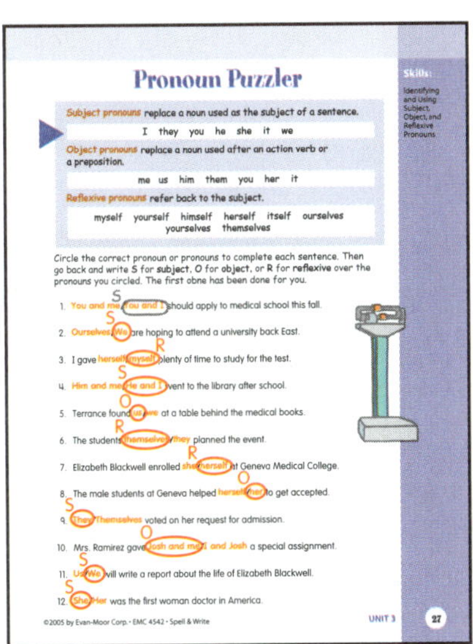

Pronoun Puzzler

Skills: Identifying and Using Subject, Object, and Reflexive Pronouns

Subject pronouns replace a noun used as the subject of a sentence.

I they you he she it we

Object pronouns replace a noun used after an action verb or a preposition.

me us him them you her it

Reflexive pronouns refer back to the subject.

myself yourself himself herself itself ourselves yourselves themselves

Circle the correct pronoun or pronouns to complete each sentence. Then go back and write S for subject, O for object, or R for reflexive over the pronouns you circled. The first one has been done for you.

1. You and me / (You and I) should apply to medical school this fall. (S)
2. Ourselves / (We) are hoping to attend a university back East. (S)
3. I gave herself / (myself) plenty of time to study for the test. (R)
4. Him and me / (He and I) went to the library after school. (S)
5. Terrance found (us) / we at a table behind the medical books. (O)
6. The students (themselves) / they planned the event. (R)
7. Elizabeth Blackwell enrolled she / (herself) at Geneva Medical College. (R)
8. The male students at Geneva helped herself / (her) to get accepted. (O)
9. (They) / Themselves voted on her request for admission. (S)
10. Mrs. Ramirez gave (Josh and me) / I and Josh a special assignment. (O)
11. Us / (We) will write a report about the life of Elizabeth Blackwell. (S)
12. (She) / Her was the first woman doctor in America. (S)

©2005 by Evan-Moor Corp. • EMC 4542 • Spell & Write UNIT 3 27

Page 28

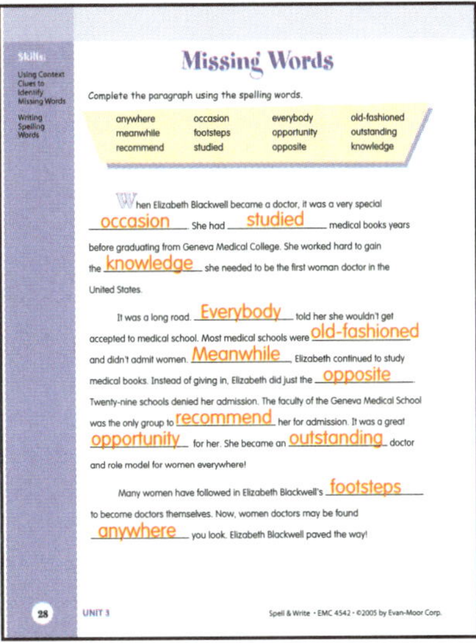

Missing Words

Skills: Using Context Clues to Identify Missing Words; Writing Spelling Words

Complete the paragraph using the spelling words.

anywhere occasion everybody old-fashioned
meanwhile footsteps opportunity outstanding
recommend studied opposite knowledge

When Elizabeth Blackwell became a doctor, it was a very special **occasion**. She had **studied** medical books years before graduating from Geneva Medical College. She worked hard to gain the **knowledge** she needed to be the first woman doctor in the United States.

It was a long road. **Everybody** told her she wouldn't get accepted to medical school. Most medical schools were **old-fashioned** and didn't admit women. **Meanwhile**, Elizabeth continued to study medical books. Instead of giving in, Elizabeth did just the **opposite**. Twenty-nine schools denied her admission. The faculty of the Geneva Medical School was the only group to **recommend** her for admission. It was a great **opportunity** for her. She became an **outstanding** doctor and role model for women everywhere!

Many women have followed in Elizabeth Blackwell's **footsteps** to become doctors themselves. Now, women doctors may be found **anywhere** you look. Elizabeth Blackwell paved the way!

28 UNIT 3 Spell & Write • EMC 4542 • ©2005 by Evan-Moor Corp.

Page 30

Poetry Time

Skills: Using Spelling Words in an Acrostic Poem

Create an acrostic poem. Write a word or phrase that starts with each letter in the topic word. Use a dictionary and words in the story to help you.

B Responses will vary.
L
A
C
K
W
E
L
L

30 UNIT 3 Spell & Write • EMC 4542 • ©2005 by Evan-Moor Corp.

Page 31

Special Firsts

Skills: Writing a Personal Narrative

Elizabeth Blackwell became the first American woman doctor in January 1849. Think of important "firsts" in your own life. Have you ever won first place in a contest or competition? Do you remember the first time you saw snow or the ocean? Write about this special "first" below. Provide lots of descriptive details.

Responses will vary.

Edit Your Work
- I used complete sentences.
- I used correct spelling.
- I used correct capitalization and punctuation.

©2005 by Evan-Moor Corp. • EMC 4542 • Spell & Write UNIT 3 31

Page 32

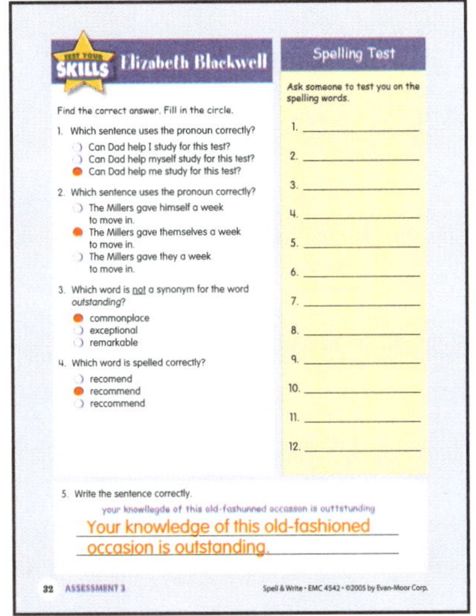

Test Your Skills — Elizabeth Blackwell

Find the correct answer. Fill in the circle.

1. Which sentence uses the pronoun correctly?
   - ○ Can Dad help I study for this test?
   - ○ Can Dad help myself study for this test?
   - ● Can Dad help me study for this test?
2. Which sentence uses the pronoun correctly?
   - ○ The Millers gave himself a week to move in.
   - ● The Millers gave themselves a week to move in.
   - ○ The Millers gave they a week to move in.
3. Which word is not a synonym for the word outstanding?
   - ● commonplace
   - ○ exceptional
   - ○ remarkable
4. Which word is spelled correctly?
   - ○ recomend
   - ● recommend
   - ○ reccommend
5. Write the sentence correctly.

   your knowlegde of this old-fashunned occasion is outtstanding

   Your knowledge of this old-fashioned occasion is outstanding.

Spelling Test

Ask someone to test you on the spelling words.

1. ______
2. ______
3. ______
4. ______
5. ______
6. ______
7. ______
8. ______
9. ______
10. ______
11. ______
12. ______

32 ASSESSMENT 3 Spell & Write • EMC 4542 • ©2005 by Evan-Moor Corp.

Page 33

Page 35

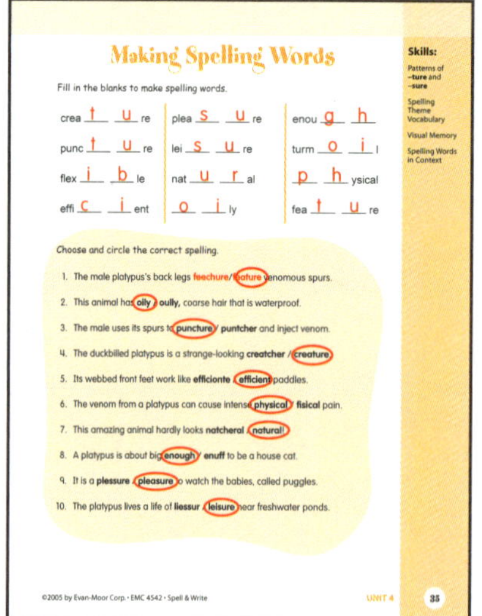

Page 36

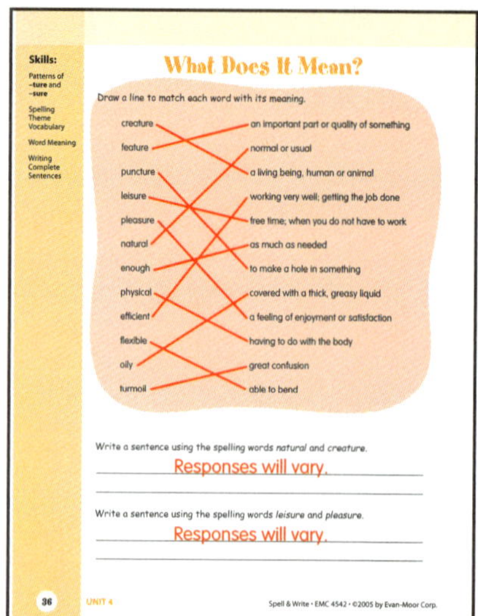

Page 37

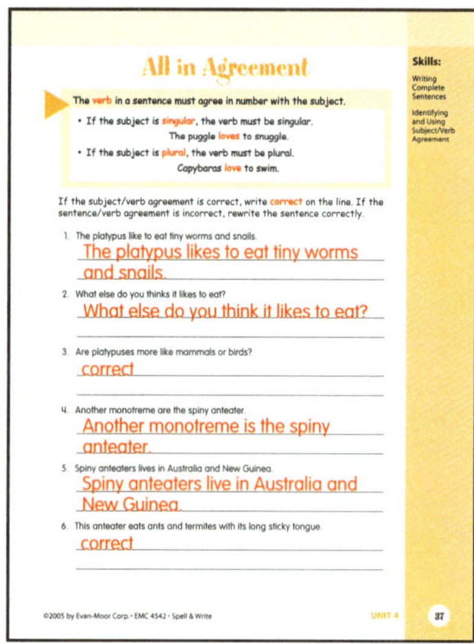

Page 38

Page 40

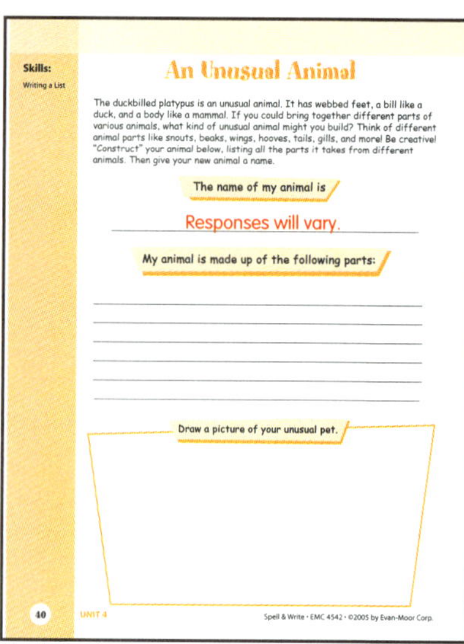

Page 41

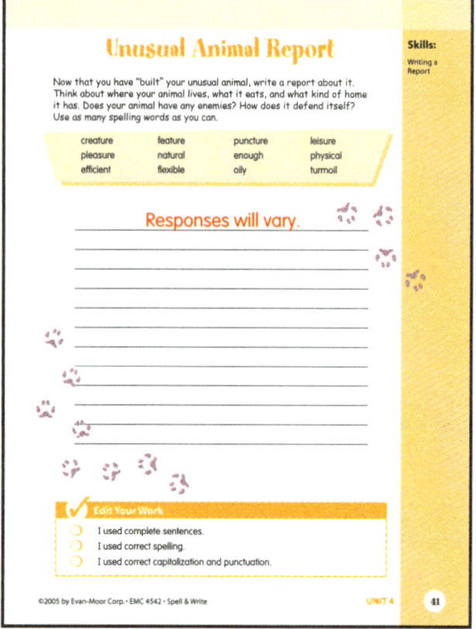

Page 42

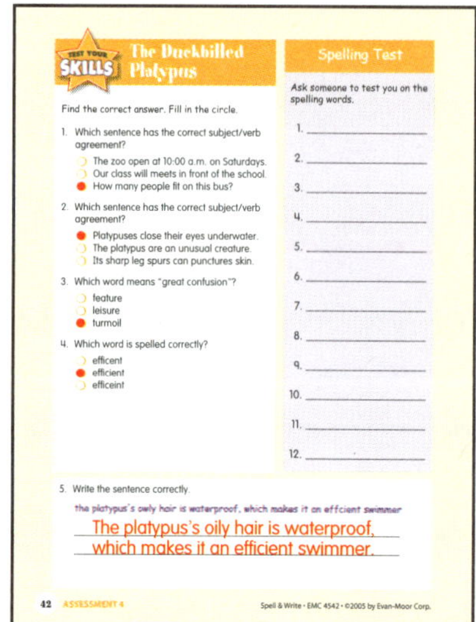

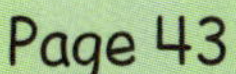

Page 43

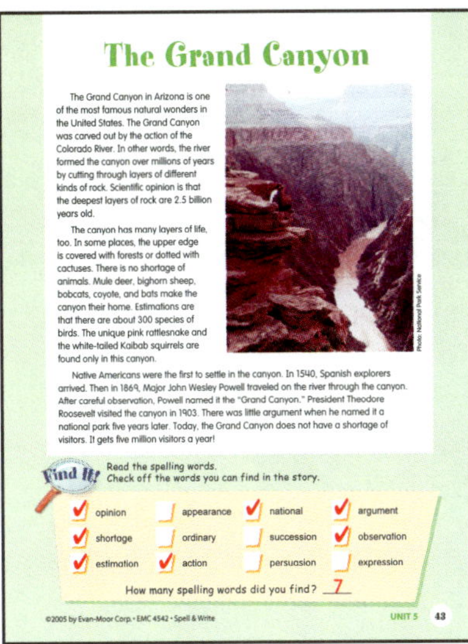

The Grand Canyon

The Grand Canyon in Arizona is one of the most famous natural wonders in the United States. The Grand Canyon was carved out by the action of the Colorado River. In other words, the river formed the canyon over millions of years by cutting through layers of different kinds of rock. Scientific opinion is that the deepest layers of rock are 2.5 billion years old.

The canyon has many layers of life, too. In some places, the upper edge is covered with forests or dotted with cactuses. There is no shortage of animals. Mule deer, bighorn sheep, bobcats, coyote, and bats make the canyon their home. Estimations are that there are about 300 species of birds. The unique pink rattlesnake and the white-tailed Kaibab squirrels are found only in this canyon.

Photo: National Park Service

Native Americans were the first to settle in the canyon. In 1540, Spanish explorers arrived. Then in 1869, Major John Wesley Powell traveled on the river through the canyon. After careful observation, Powell named it the "Grand Canyon." President Theodore Roosevelt visited the canyon in 1903. There was little argument when he named it a national park five years later. Today, the Grand Canyon does not have a shortage of visitors. It gets five million visitors a year!

Find It! Read the spelling words. Check off the words you can find in the story.

✔ opinion	appearance	✔ national	✔ argument
✔ shortage	ordinary	succession	✔ observation
✔ estimation	✔ action	persuasion	expression

How many spelling words did you find? 7

©2005 by Evan-Moor Corp. • EMC 4542 • Spell & Write UNIT 5 43

Page 45

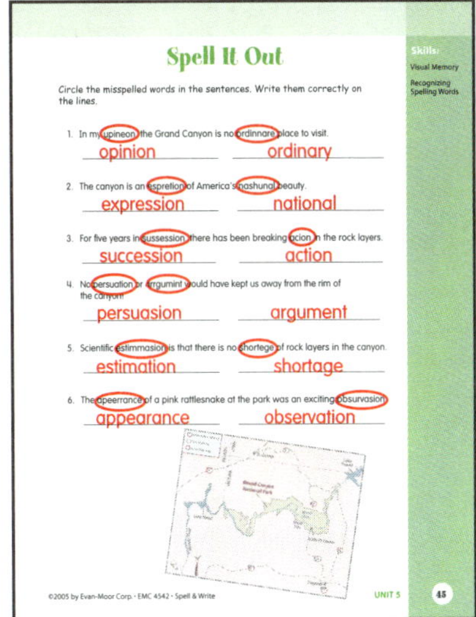

Spell It Out

Skills: Visual Memory; Recognizing Spelling Words

Circle the misspelled words in the sentences. Write them correctly on the lines.

1. In my upineon the Grand Canyon is no ordinnare place to visit.
   opinion ordinary
2. The canyon is an espretion of America's nashunal beauty.
   expression national
3. For five years in sussession there has been breaking acion in the rock layers.
   succession action
4. No persuation or arrgumint would have kept us away from the rim of the canyon!
   persuasion argument
5. Scientific estimmasion is that there is no shortege of rock layers in the canyon.
   estimation shortage
6. The apeerrance of a pink rattlesnake at the park was an exciting obsurvasion.
   appearance observation

©2005 by Evan-Moor Corp. • EMC 4542 • Spell & Write UNIT 5 45

Page 46

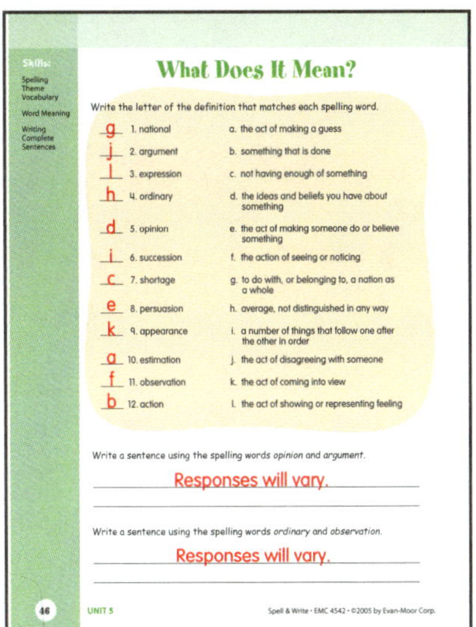

What Does It Mean?

Skills: Spelling Theme Vocabulary; Word Meaning; Writing Complete Sentences

Write the letter of the definition that matches each spelling word.

g	1. national	a. the act of making a guess
j	2. argument	b. something that is done
l	3. expression	c. not having enough of something
h	4. ordinary	d. the ideas and beliefs you have about something
d	5. opinion	e. the act of making someone do or believe something
i	6. succession	f. the action of seeing or noticing
c	7. shortage	g. to do with, or belonging to, a nation as a whole
e	8. persuasion	h. average, not distinguished in any way
k	9. appearance	i. a number of things that follow one after the other in order
a	10. estimation	j. the act of disagreeing with someone
f	11. observation	k. the act of coming into view
b	12. action	l. the act of showing or representing feeling

Write a sentence using the spelling words *opinion* and *argument*.

Responses will vary.

Write a sentence using the spelling words *ordinary* and *observation*.

Responses will vary.

46 UNIT 5 Spell & Write • EMC 4542 • ©2005 by Evan-Moor Corp.

Page 47

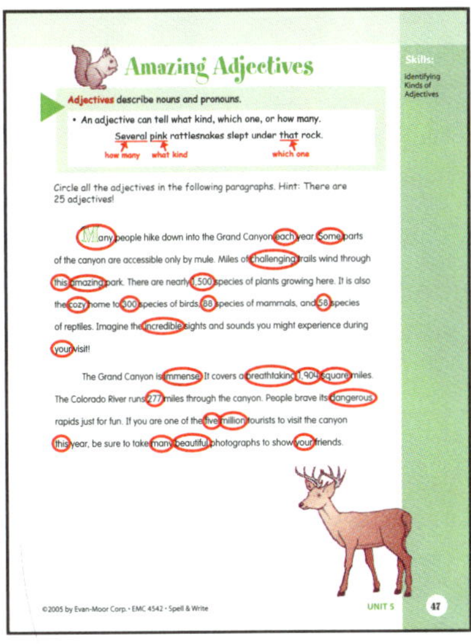

Amazing Adjectives

Skills: Identifying Kinds of Adjectives

Adjectives describe nouns and pronouns.

- An adjective can tell what kind, which one, or how many.

  Several pink rattlesnakes slept under that rock.
  (Several: how many; pink: what kind; that: which one)

Circle all the adjectives in the following paragraphs. Hint: There are 25 adjectives!

Many people hike down into the Grand Canyon each year. Some parts of the canyon are accessible only by mule. Miles of challenging trails wind through this amazing park. There are nearly 1,500 species of plants growing here. It is also the cozy home to 300 species of birds, 88 species of mammals, and 58 species of reptiles. Imagine the incredible sights and sounds you might experience during your visit!

The Grand Canyon is immense. It covers a breathtaking 1,904 square miles. The Colorado River runs 277 miles through the canyon. People brave its dangerous rapids just for fun. If you are one of the five million tourists to visit the canyon this year, be sure to take many beautiful photographs to show your friends.

©2005 by Evan-Moor Corp. • EMC 4542 • Spell & Write UNIT 5 47

Page 48

Word Search

Skills: Visual Sequencing; Recognizing Spelling Words

Find and circle the spelling words. Words can go across, down, or diagonally.

opinion	appearance	national	argument
shortage	ordinary	succession	observation
estimation	action	persuasion	expression

C I O N B I E W D A Y T B
M Y P E R S U A S I O N T
E C N O I S S E R P X E N
N K L A N O I T A N G M E
T A G E Q Z M Q O L J U E
S U C C E S S I O N O G C
H N A T W Q T U R Z N R N
O Y B D R A K N D O P A A
R C H N M V O V I I G D R
T W J I Q I U T N C L H A
A B T K N L C N A C J B E
G S E I A A D F R U W A P
E A P P E A A R Y S Y Z P
Z O B S E R V A T I O N A

48 UNIT 5 Spell & Write • EMC 4542 • ©2005 by Evan-Moor Corp.

Page 50

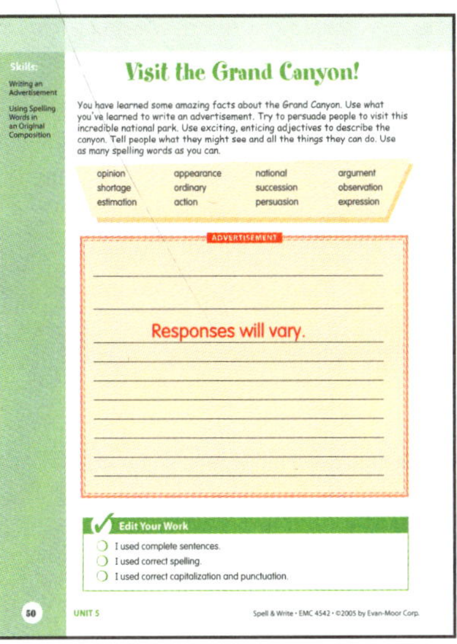

Visit the Grand Canyon!

Skills: Writing an Advertisement; Using Spelling Words in an Original Composition

You have learned some amazing facts about the Grand Canyon. Use what you've learned to write an advertisement. Try to persuade people to visit this incredible national park. Use exciting, enticing adjectives to describe the canyon. Tell people what they might see and all the things they can do. Use as many spelling words as you can.

opinion	appearance	national	argument
shortage	ordinary	succession	observation
estimation	action	persuasion	expression

ADVERTISEMENT

Responses will vary.

Edit Your Work

- I used complete sentences.
- I used correct spelling.
- I used correct capitalization and punctuation.

50 UNIT 5 Spell & Write • EMC 4542 • ©2005 by Evan-Moor Corp.

Page 51

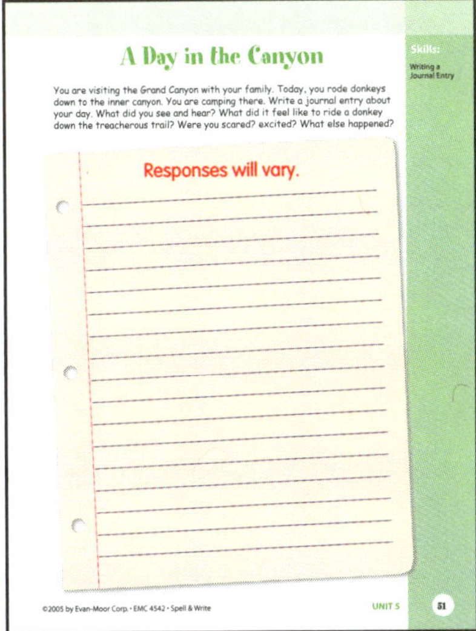

A Day in the Canyon

Skills: Writing a Journal Entry

You are visiting the Grand Canyon with your family. Today, you rode donkeys down to the inner canyon. You are camping there. Write a journal entry about your day. What did you see and hear? What did it feel like to ride a donkey down the treacherous trail? Were you scared? excited? What else happened?

Responses will vary.

©2005 by Evan-Moor Corp. • EMC 4542 • Spell & Write UNIT 5 51

Page 52

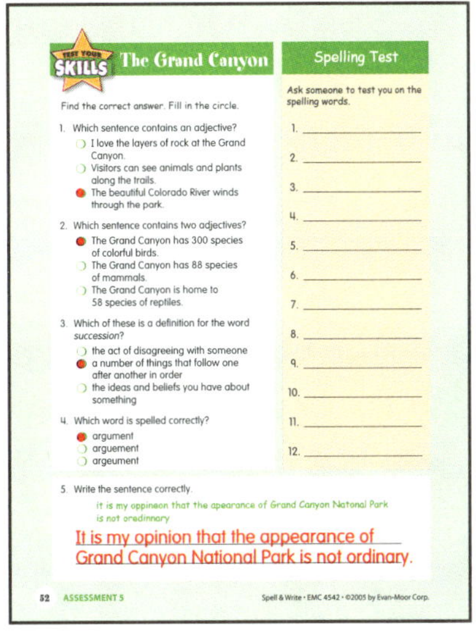

Test Your Skills: The Grand Canyon

Find the correct answer. Fill in the circle.

1. Which sentence contains an adjective?
   - ○ I love the layers of rock at the Grand Canyon.
   - ○ Visitors can see animals and plants along the trails.
   - ● The beautiful Colorado River winds through the park.
2. Which sentence contains two adjectives?
   - ● The Grand Canyon has 300 species of colorful birds.
   - ○ The Grand Canyon has 88 species of mammals.
   - ○ The Grand Canyon is home to 58 species of reptiles.
3. Which of these is a definition for the word *succession*?
   - ○ the act of disagreeing with someone
   - ● a number of things that follow one after another in order
   - ○ the ideas and beliefs you have about something
4. Which word is spelled correctly?
   - ● argument
   - ○ arguement
   - ○ argeument
5. Write the sentence correctly.

   it is my oppineon that the apearance of Grand Canyon Natonal Park is not oredinnary

   It is my opinion that the appearance of Grand Canyon National Park is not ordinary.

Spelling Test

Ask someone to test you on the spelling words.

1.
2.
3.
4.
5.
6.
7.
8.
9.
10.
11.
12.

52 ASSESSMENT 5 Spell & Write • EMC 4542 • ©2005 by Evan-Moor Corp.

Page 53

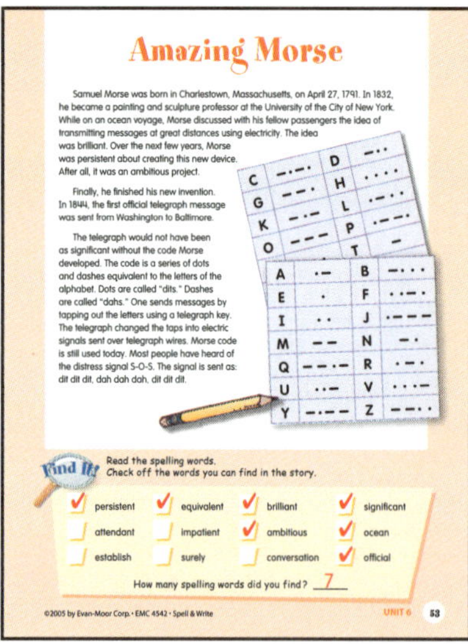

Amazing Morse

Samuel Morse was born in Charlestown, Massachusetts, on April 27, 1791. In 1832, he became a painting and sculpture professor at the University of the City of New York. While on an ocean voyage, Morse discussed with his fellow passengers the idea of transmitting messages at great distances using electricity. The idea was brilliant. Over the next few years, Morse was persistent about creating this new device. After all, it was an ambitious project.

Finally, he finished his new invention. In 1844, the first official telegraph message was sent from Washington to Baltimore.

The telegraph would not have been as significant without the code Morse developed. The code is a series of dots and dashes equivalent to the letters of the alphabet. Dots are called "dits." Dashes are called "dahs." One sends messages by tapping out the letters using a telegraph key. The telegraph changed the taps into electric signals sent over telegraph wires. Morse code is still used today. Most people have heard of the distress signal S-O-S. The signal is sent as: dit dit dit, dah dah dah, dit dit dit.

Find It! Read the spelling words. Check off the words you can find in the story.

- ✔ persistent
- ✔ equivalent
- ✔ brilliant
- ✔ significant
- attendant
- impatient
- ✔ ambitious
- ✔ ocean
- establish
- surely
- conversation
- ✔ official

How many spelling words did you find? 7

©2005 by Evan-Moor Corp. • EMC 4542 • Spell & Write UNIT 6 53

Page 55

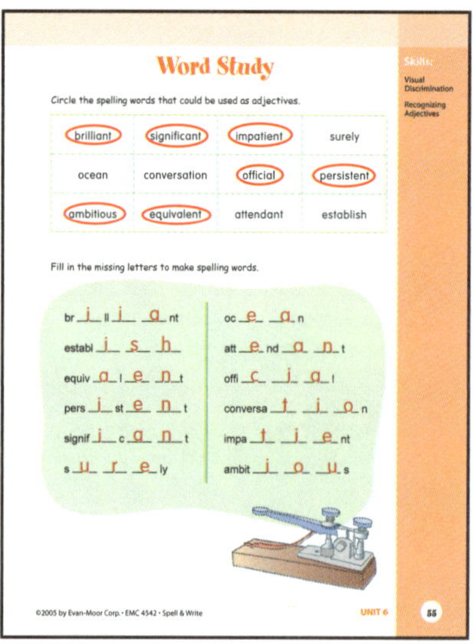

Word Study

Skills: Visual Discrimination; Recognizing Adjectives

Circle the spelling words that could be used as adjectives.

(brilliant)	(significant)	(impatient)	surely
ocean	conversation	(official)	(persistent)
(ambitious)	(equivalent)	attendant	establish

Fill in the missing letters to make spelling words.

brilliant	ocean
establish	attendant
equivalent	official
persistent	conversation
significant	impatient
surely	ambitious

©2005 by Evan-Moor Corp. • EMC 4542 • Spell & Write UNIT 6 55

Page 56

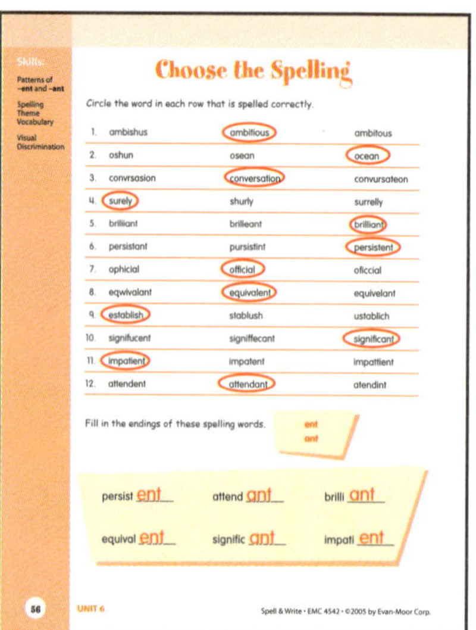

Choose the Spelling

Skills: Patterns of -ent and -ant; Spelling Theme Vocabulary; Visual Discrimination

Circle the word in each row that is spelled correctly.

1.	ambishus	(ambitious)	ambitous
2.	oshun	osean	(ocean)
3.	convrsasion	(conversation)	convursateon
4.	(surely)	shurly	surrelly
5.	brilliant	brilleant	(brilliant)
6.	persistant	pursistint	(persistent)
7.	ophicial	(official)	oficcial
8.	eqwivalant	(equivalent)	equivelant
9.	(establish)	stablush	ustablich
10.	signifucent	signiffecant	(significant)
11.	(impatient)	impatent	impattient
12.	attendent	(attendant)	atendint

Fill in the endings of these spelling words. ent / ant

persist ent   attend ant   brilli ant

equival ent   signific ant   impati ent

56 UNIT 6 Spell & Write • EMC 4542 • ©2005 by Evan-Moor Corp.

Page 57

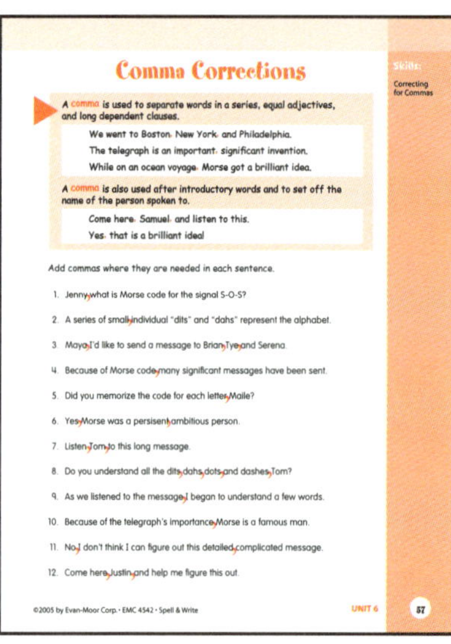

Comma Corrections

Skills: Correcting for Commas

A comma is used to separate words in a series, equal adjectives, and long dependent clauses.

We went to Boston, New York, and Philadelphia.
The telegraph is an important, significant invention.
While on an ocean voyage, Morse got a brilliant idea.

A comma is also used after introductory words and to set off the name of the person spoken to.

Come here, Samuel, and listen to this.
Yes, that is a brilliant idea!

Add commas where they are needed in each sentence.

1. Jenny, what is Morse code for the signal S-O-S?
2. A series of small, individual "dits" and "dahs" represent the alphabet.
3. Maya, I'd like to send a message to Brian, Tye, and Serena.
4. Because of Morse code, many significant messages have been sent.
5. Did you memorize the code for each letter, Maile?
6. Yes, Morse was a persisent, ambitious person.
7. Listen, Tom, to this long message.
8. Do you understand all the dits, dahs, dots, and dashes, Tom?
9. As we listened to the message, I began to understand a few words.
10. Because of the telegraph's importance, Morse is a famous man.
11. No, I don't think I can figure out this detailed, complicated message.
12. Come here, Justin, and help me figure this out.

©2005 by Evan-Moor Corp. • EMC 4542 • Spell & Write UNIT 6 57

Page 58

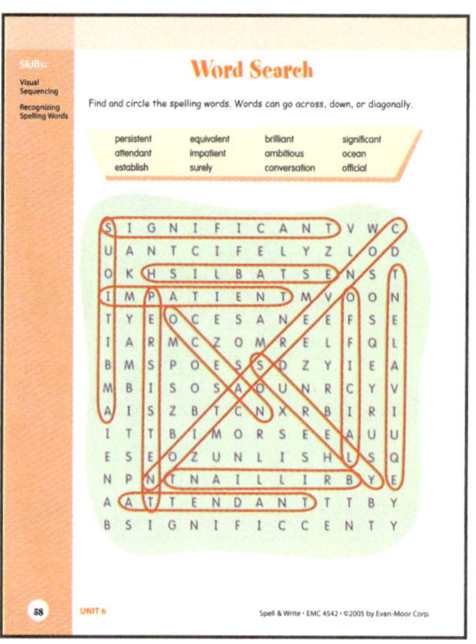

Word Search

Skills: Visual Sequencing; Recognizing Spelling Words

Find and circle the spelling words. Words can go across, down, or diagonally.

persistent	equivalent	brilliant	significant
attendant	impatient	ambitious	ocean
establish	surely	conversation	official

58 UNIT 6 Spell & Write • EMC 4542 • ©2005 by Evan-Moor Corp.

Page 60

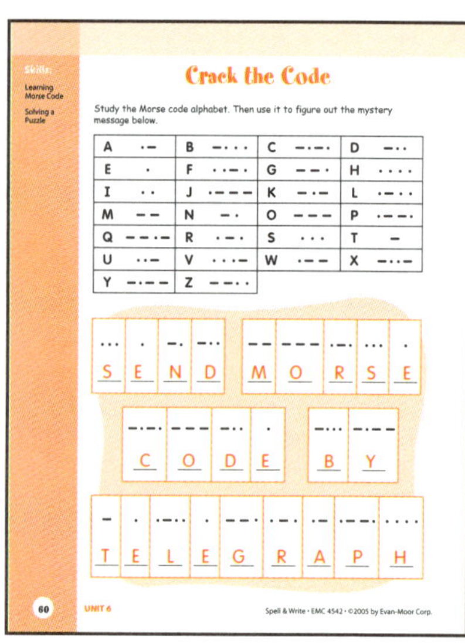

Crack the Code

Skills: Learning Morse Code; Solving a Puzzle

Study the Morse code alphabet. Then use it to figure out the mystery message below.

A	·–	B	–···	C	–·–·	D	–··
E	·	F	··–·	G	––·	H	····
I	··	J	·–––	K	–·–	L	·–··
M	––	N	–·	O	–––	P	·––·
Q	––·–	R	·–·	S	···	T	–
U	··–	V	···–	W	·––	X	–··–
Y	–·––	Z	––··				

SEND MORSE
CODE BY
TELEGRAPH

60 UNIT 6 Spell & Write • EMC 4542 • ©2005 by Evan-Moor Corp.

Page 61

Morse Code Message

Skills: Writing a Morse Code Message

Now that you know Morse code, send your own message! Think of a friend to whom you'd like to send a message. Fill in each box with a letter from the code on page 60. Draw a vertical line between boxes to separate words. Then give your message to a friend to solve!

Responses will vary.

©2005 by Evan-Moor Corp. • EMC 4542 • Spell & Write UNIT 6 61

Page 62

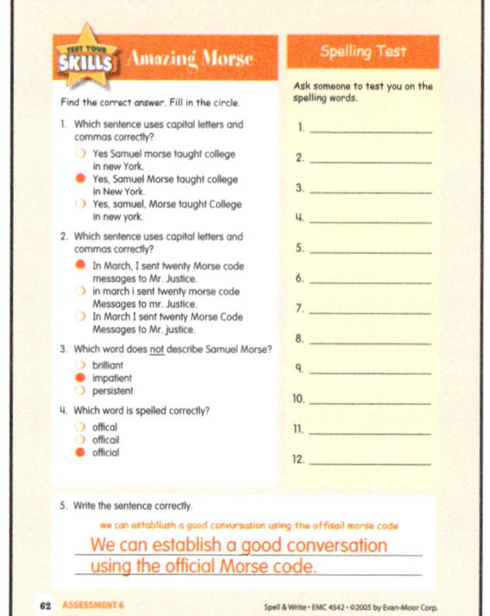

TEST YOUR SKILLS Amazing Morse

Find the correct answer. Fill in the circle.

1. Which sentence uses capital letters and commas correctly?
   - ○ Yes Samuel morse taught college in new York.
   - ● Yes, Samuel Morse taught college in New York.
   - ○ Yes, samuel, Morse taught College in new york.
2. Which sentence uses capital letters and commas correctly?
   - ● In March, I sent twenty Morse code messages to Mr. Justice.
   - ○ in march i sent twenty morse code Messages to mr. Justice.
   - ○ In March I sent twenty Morse Code Messages to Mr. justice.
3. Which word does not describe Samuel Morse?
   - ○ brilliant
   - ● impatient
   - ○ persistent
4. Which word is spelled correctly?
   - ○ offical
   - ○ officail
   - ● official
5. Write the sentence correctly.

   we can establlush a good convursasion using the offisail morse code

   We can establish a good conversation using the official Morse code.

Spelling Test

Ask someone to test you on the spelling words.

1. ____
2. ____
3. ____
4. ____
5. ____
6. ____
7. ____
8. ____
9. ____
10. ____
11. ____
12. ____

62 ASSESSMENT 6 Spell & Write • EMC 4542 • ©2005 by Evan-Moor Corp.

Page 63

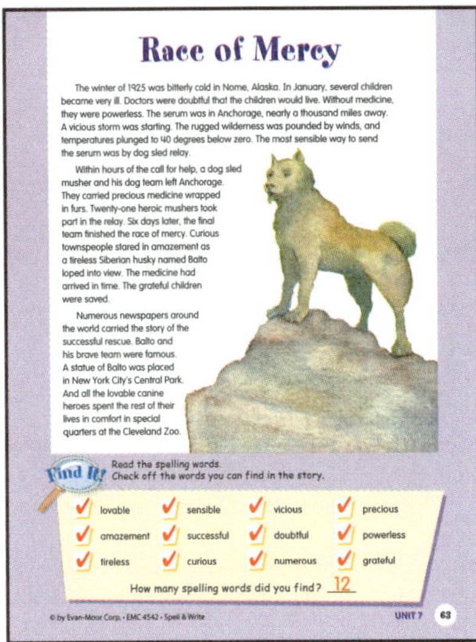

Race of Mercy

The winter of 1925 was bitterly cold in Nome, Alaska. In January, several children became very ill. Doctors were doubtful that the children would live. Without medicine, they were powerless. The serum was in Anchorage, nearly a thousand miles away. A vicious storm was starting. The rugged wilderness was pounded by winds, and temperatures plunged to 40 degrees below zero. The most sensible way to send the serum was by dog sled relay.

Within hours of the call for help, a dog sled musher and his dog team left Anchorage. They carried precious medicine wrapped in furs. Twenty-one heroic mushers took part in the relay. Six days later, the final team finished the race of mercy. Curious townspeople stared in amazement as a tireless Siberian husky named Balto loped into view. The medicine had arrived in time. The grateful children were saved.

Numerous newspapers around the world carried the story of the successful rescue. Balto and his brave team were famous. A statue of Balto was placed in New York City's Central Park. And all the lovable canine heroes spent the rest of their lives in comfort in special quarters at the Cleveland Zoo.

Find It! Read the spelling words. Check off the words you can find in the story.

✓ lovable	✓ sensible	✓ vicious	✓ precious
✓ amazement	✓ successful	✓ doubtful	✓ powerless
✓ tireless	✓ curious	✓ numerous	✓ grateful

How many spelling words did you find? 12

© by Evan-Moor Corp. • EMC 4542 • Spell & Write UNIT 7 63

Page 65

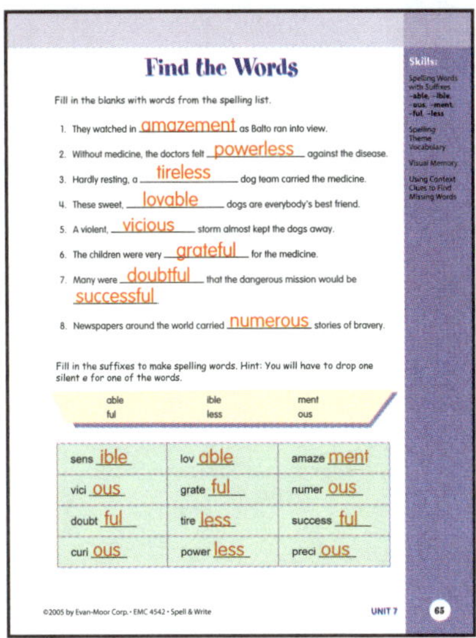

Find the Words

Skills: Spelling Words with Suffixes -able, -ible, -ous, -ment, -ful, -less; Spelling Theme Vocabulary; Visual Memory; Using Context Clues to Find Missing Words

Fill in the blanks with words from the spelling list.

1. They watched in amazement as Balto ran into view.
2. Without medicine, the doctors felt powerless against the disease.
3. Hardly resting, a tireless dog team carried the medicine.
4. These sweet, lovable dogs are everybody's best friend.
5. A violent, vicious storm almost kept the dogs away.
6. The children were very grateful for the medicine.
7. Many were doubtful that the dangerous mission would be successful.
8. Newspapers around the world carried numerous stories of bravery.

Fill in the suffixes to make spelling words. Hint: You will have to drop one silent e for one of the words.

able ible ment ful less ous

sens ible	lov able	amaze ment
vici ous	grate ful	numer ous
doubt ful	tire less	success ful
curi ous	power less	preci ous

©2005 by Evan-Moor Corp. • EMC 4542 • Spell & Write UNIT 7 65

Page 66

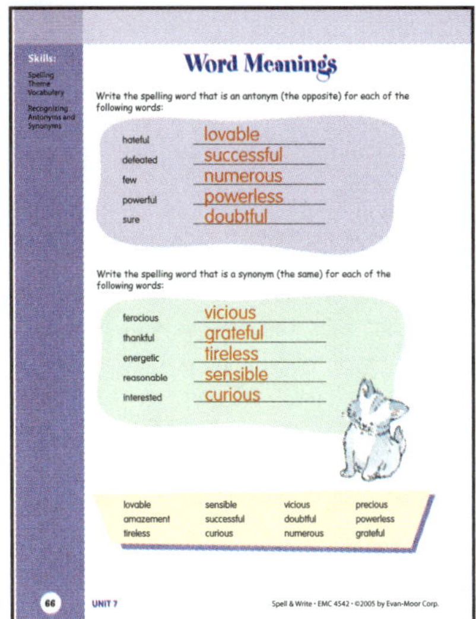

Word Meanings

Skills: Spelling Theme Vocabulary; Recognizing Antonyms and Synonyms

Write the spelling word that is an antonym (the opposite) for each of the following words:

hateful	lovable
defeated	successful
few	numerous
powerful	powerless
sure	doubtful

Write the spelling word that is a synonym (the same) for each of the following words:

ferocious	vicious
thankful	grateful
energetic	tireless
reasonable	sensible
interested	curious

lovable, sensible, vicious, precious, amazement, successful, doubtful, powerless, tireless, curious, numerous, grateful

66 UNIT 7 Spell & Write • EMC 4542 • ©2005 by Evan-Moor Corp.

Page 67

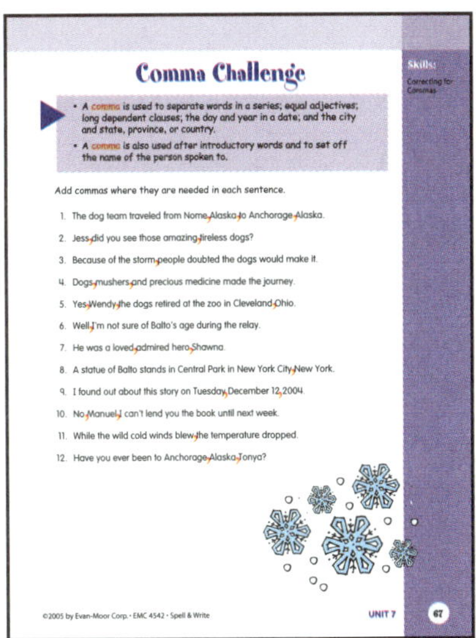

Comma Challenge

Skills: Correcting for Commas

- A comma is used to separate words in a series; equal adjectives; long dependent clauses; the day and year in a date; and the city and state, province, or country.
- A comma is also used after introductory words and to set off the name of the person spoken to.

Add commas where they are needed in each sentence.

1. The dog team traveled from Nome, Alaska, to Anchorage, Alaska.
2. Jess, did you see those amazing, tireless dogs?
3. Because of the storm, people doubted the dogs would make it.
4. Dogs, mushers, and precious medicine made the journey.
5. Yes, Wendy, the dogs retired at the zoo in Cleveland, Ohio.
6. Well, I'm not sure of Balto's age during the relay.
7. He was a loved, admired hero, Shawna.
8. A statue of Balto stands in Central Park in New York City, New York.
9. I found out about this story on Tuesday, December 12, 2004.
10. No, Manuel, I can't lend you the book until next week.
11. While the wild cold winds blew, the temperature dropped.
12. Have you ever been to Anchorage, Alaska, Tonya?

©2005 by Evan-Moor Corp. • EMC 4542 • Spell & Write UNIT 7 67

Page 68

Secret Code

Skills: Visual Discrimination; Using Spelling Words

Write the letter that stands for each number to discover six of the spelling words.

a	b	c	d	e	f	g	i	l	m	n	o	p	r	s	t	u	v	w
1	2	3	4	5	6	7	8	9	10	11	12	13	14	15	16	17	18	19

1. v i c i o u s (18 8 3 8 12 17 15)
2. c u r i o u s (3 17 14 8 12 17 15)
3. p r e c i o u s (13 14 5 3 8 12 17 15)
4. n u m e r o u s (11 17 10 5 14 12 17 15)
5. p o w e r l e s s (13 12 19 5 14 9 5 15 15)
6. s u c c e s s f u l (15 17 3 3 5 15 15 6 17 9)

68 UNIT 7 Spell & Write • EMC 4542 • ©2005 by Evan-Moor Corp.

Page 70

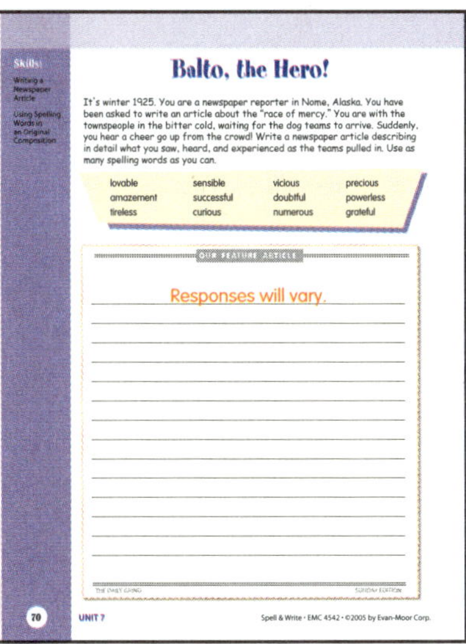

Balto, the Hero!

Skills: Writing a Newspaper Article; Using Spelling Words in an Original Composition

It's winter 1925. You are a newspaper reporter in Nome, Alaska. You have been asked to write an article about the "race of mercy." You are with the townspeople in the bitter cold, waiting for the dog teams to arrive. Suddenly, you hear a cheer go up from the crowd! Write a newspaper article describing in detail what you saw, heard, and experienced as the teams pulled in. Use as many spelling words as you can.

lovable, sensible, vicious, precious, amazement, successful, doubtful, powerless, tireless, curious, numerous, grateful

OUR FEATURE ARTICLE

Responses will vary.

70 UNIT 7 Spell & Write • EMC 4542 • ©2005 by Evan-Moor Corp.

Page 71

Animal Heroes

Skills: Writing a Creative Story

Have you ever heard of other animal heroes besides Balto? Cats have been known to warn their owners of a burning house. Dogs have found lost people just by scent. Write a story about an animal that did a heroic deed. What happened, and how did the animal save the day?

Responses will vary.

Edit Your Work

- I used complete sentences.
- I used correct spelling.
- I used correct capitalization and punctuation.

©2005 by Evan-Moor Corp. • EMC 4542 • Spell & Write UNIT 7 71

Page 72

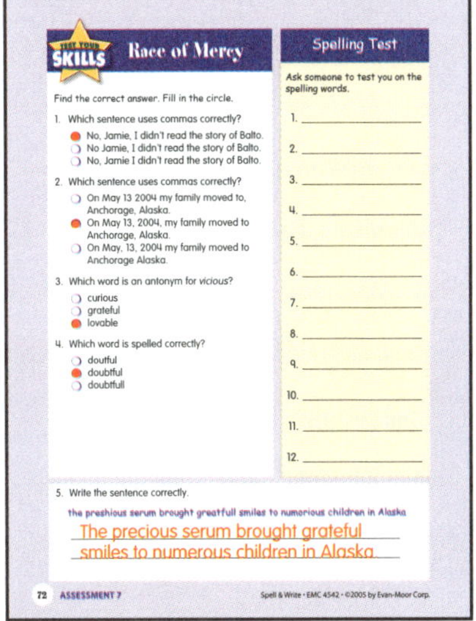

Test Your Skills: Race of Mercy

Find the correct answer. Fill in the circle.

1. Which sentence uses commas correctly?
   - ● No, Jamie, I didn't read the story of Balto.
   - ○ No Jamie, I didn't read the story of Balto.
   - ○ No, Jamie I didn't read the story of Balto.
2. Which sentence uses commas correctly?
   - ○ On May 13 2004 my family moved to, Anchorage, Alaska.
   - ● On May 13, 2004, my family moved to Anchorage, Alaska.
   - ○ On May, 13, 2004 my family moved to Anchorage Alaska.
3. Which word is an antonym for vicious?
   - ○ curious
   - ○ grateful
   - ● lovable
4. Which word is spelled correctly?
   - ○ doutful
   - ● doubtful
   - ○ doubtfull
5. Write the sentence correctly.

   the preshious serum brought greatfull smiles to numorious children in Alaska

   The precious serum brought grateful smiles to numerous children in Alaska.

Spelling Test

Ask someone to test you on the spelling words.

1. ______
2. ______
3. ______
4. ______
5. ______
6. ______
7. ______
8. ______
9. ______
10. ______
11. ______
12. ______

72 ASSESSMENT 7 Spell & Write • EMC 4542 • ©2005 by Evan-Moor Corp.

Page 73

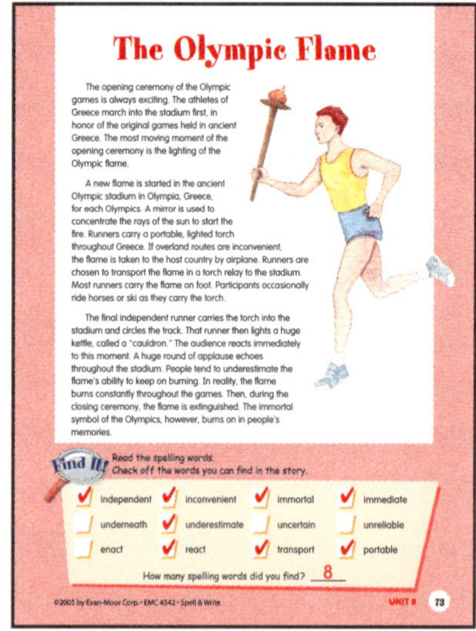

The Olympic Flame

The opening ceremony of the Olympic games is always exciting. The athletes of Greece march into the stadium first, in honor of the original games held in ancient Greece. The most moving moment of the opening ceremony is the lighting of the Olympic flame.

A new flame is started in the ancient Olympic stadium in Olympia, Greece, for each Olympics. A mirror is used to concentrate the rays of the sun to start the fire. Runners carry a portable, lighted torch throughout Greece. If overland routes are inconvenient, the flame is taken to the host country by airplane. Runners are chosen to transport the flame in a torch relay to the stadium. Most runners carry the flame on foot. Participants occasionally ride horses or ski as they carry the torch.

The final independent runner carries the torch into the stadium and circles the track. That runner then lights a huge kettle, called a "cauldron." The audience reacts immediately to this moment. A huge round of applause echoes throughout the stadium. People tend to underestimate the flame's ability to keep on burning. In reality, the flame burns constantly throughout the games. Then, during the closing ceremony, the flame is extinguished. The immortal symbol of the Olympics, however, burns on in people's memories.

Find It! Read the spelling words. Check off the words you can find in the story.

✓ independent	✓ inconvenient	✓ immortal	✓ immediate
underneath	✓ underestimate	uncertain	unreliable
enact	✓ react	✓ transport	✓ portable

How many spelling words did you find? 8

©2005 by Evan-Moor Corp. • EMC 4542 • Spell & Write UNIT 8 73

Page 75

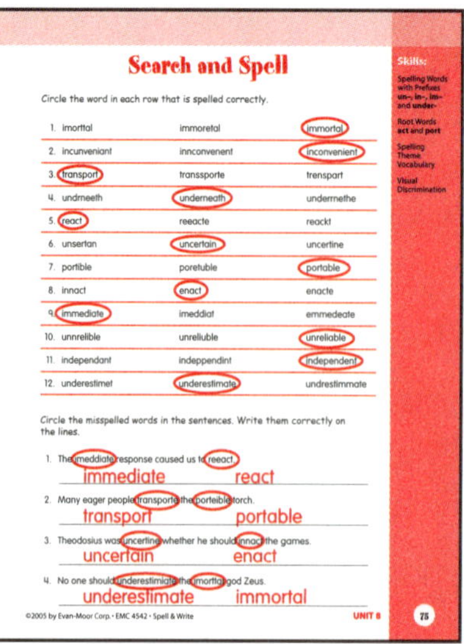

Search and Spell

Skills: Spelling Words with Prefixes un-, in-, im-, and under-; Root Words act and port; Spelling Theme Vocabulary; Visual Discrimination

Circle the word in each row that is spelled correctly.

1.	imortal	immoretal	(immortal)
2.	incunvenient	innconvenent	(inconvenient)
3.	(transport)	transsporte	trensport
4.	undrneeth	(underneath)	undernethe
5.	(react)	reeacte	reackt
6.	unsertan	(uncertain)	uncertine
7.	portible	poretuble	(portable)
8.	innact	(enact)	enacte
9.	(immediate)	imeddiat	emmedeate
10.	unrrelible	unreliuble	(unreliable)
11.	independant	indeppendint	(independent)
12.	underestimet	(underestimate)	undrestimmate

Circle the misspelled words in the sentences. Write them correctly on the lines.

1. The (imeddiate) response caused us to (reeact). immediate react
2. Many eager people (transporte) the (porteible) torch. transport portable
3. Theodosius was (uncertine) whether he should (innact) the games. uncertain enact
4. No one should (underestimate) the (imortal) god Zeus. underestimate immortal

©2005 by Evan-Moor Corp. • EMC 4542 • Spell & Write UNIT 8 75

Page 76

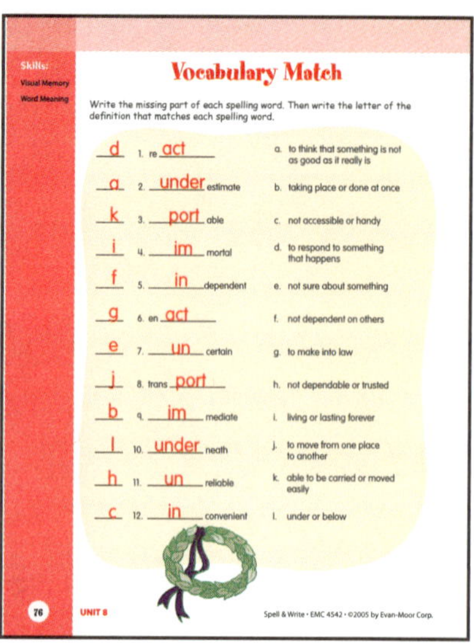

Vocabulary Match

Skills: Visual Memory; Word Meaning

Write the missing part of each spelling word. Then write the letter of the definition that matches each spelling word.

d	1. re act	a. to think that something is not as good as it really is
a	2. under estimate	b. taking place or done at once
k	3. port able	c. not accessible or handy
i	4. im mortal	d. to respond to something that happens
f	5. in dependent	e. not sure about something
g	6. en act	f. not dependent on others
e	7. un certain	g. to make into law
j	8. trans port	h. not dependable or trusted
b	9. im mediate	i. living or lasting forever
l	10. under neath	j. to move from one place to another
h	11. un reliable	k. able to be carried or moved easily
c	12. in convenient	l. under or below

76 UNIT 8 Spell & Write • EMC 4542 • ©2005 by Evan-Moor Corp.

Page 77

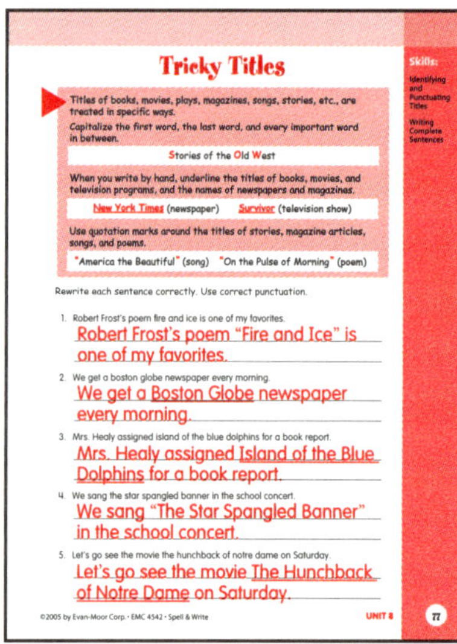

Tricky Titles

Skills: Identifying and Punctuating Titles; Writing Complete Sentences

Titles of books, movies, plays, magazines, songs, stories, etc., are treated in specific ways.

Capitalize the first word, the last word, and every important word in between.

Stories of the Old West

When you write by hand, underline the titles of books, movies, and television programs, and the names of newspapers and magazines.

New York Times (newspaper) Survivor (television show)

Use quotation marks around the titles of stories, magazine articles, songs, and poems.

"America the Beautiful" (song) "On the Pulse of Morning" (poem)

Rewrite each sentence correctly. Use correct punctuation.

1. Robert Frost's poem fire and ice is one of my favorites.
   Robert Frost's poem "Fire and Ice" is one of my favorites.
2. We get a boston globe newspaper every morning.
   We get a Boston Globe newspaper every morning.
3. Mrs. Healy assigned island of the blue dolphins for a book report.
   Mrs. Healy assigned Island of the Blue Dolphins for a book report.
4. We sang the star spangled banner in the school concert.
   We sang "The Star Spangled Banner" in the school concert.
5. Let's go see the movie the hunchback of notre dame on Saturday.
   Let's go see the movie The Hunchback of Notre Dame on Saturday.

©2005 by Evan-Moor Corp. • EMC 4542 • Spell & Write UNIT 8 77

Page 78

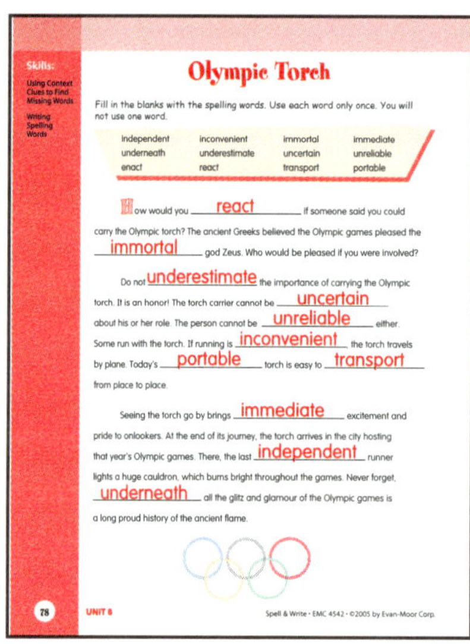

Olympic Torch

Skills: Using Context Clues to Find Missing Words; Writing Spelling Words

Fill in the blanks with the spelling words. Use each word only once. You will not use one word.

independent	inconvenient	immortal	immediate
underneath	underestimate	uncertain	unreliable
enact	react	transport	portable

How would you react if someone said you could carry the Olympic torch? The ancient Greeks believed the Olympic games pleased the immortal god Zeus. Who would be pleased if you were involved?

Do not underestimate the importance of carrying the Olympic torch. It is an honor! The torch carrier cannot be uncertain about his or her role. The person cannot be unreliable either. Some run with the torch. If running is inconvenient, the torch travels by plane. Today's portable torch is easy to transport from place to place.

Seeing the torch go by brings immediate excitement and pride to onlookers. At the end of its journey, the torch arrives in the city hosting that year's Olympic games. There, the last independent runner lights a huge cauldron, which burns bright throughout the games. Never forget, underneath all the glitz and glamour of the Olympic games is a long proud history of the ancient flame.

78 UNIT 8 Spell & Write • EMC 4542 • ©2005 by Evan-Moor Corp.

Page 80

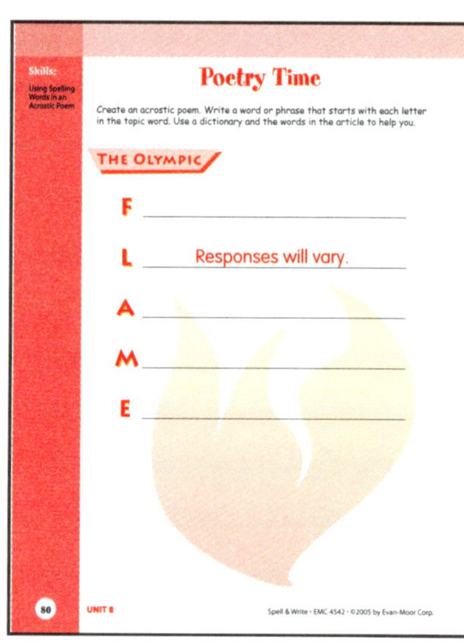

Poetry Time

Skills: Using Spelling Words in an Acrostic Poem

Create an acrostic poem. Write a word or phrase that starts with each letter in the topic word. Use a dictionary and the words in the article to help you.

THE OLYMPIC

F
L Responses will vary.
A
M
E

80 UNIT 8 Spell & Write • EMC 4542 • ©2005 by Evan-Moor Corp.

Page 81

Carrying the Torch

Skills: Writing a Friendly Letter

You have been asked to carry the Olympic torch through your hometown or city. What do you think it will be like? Will crowds cheer for you? How will you feel? Write a letter to a friend, telling about your experience carrying the Olympic torch.

Responses will vary.

Your friend,

Edit Your Work

- I used complete sentences.
- I used correct spelling.
- I used correct capitalization and punctuation.

©2005 by Evan-Moor Corp. • EMC 4542 • Spell & Write UNIT 8 81

Page 82

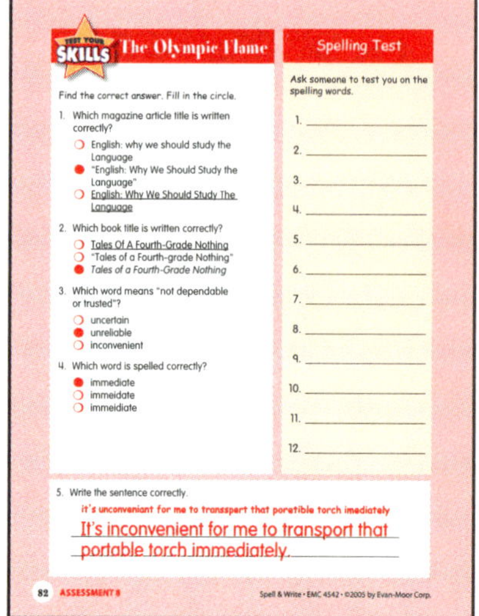

Test Your Skills: The Olympic Flame

Find the correct answer. Fill in the circle.

1. Which magazine article title is written correctly?
   - English: why we should study the Language
   - ● "English: Why We Should Study the Language"
   - English: Why We Should Study The Language
2. Which book title is written correctly?
   - Tales Of A Fourth-Grade Nothing
   - "Tales of a Fourth-grade Nothing"
   - ● *Tales of a Fourth-Grade Nothing*
3. Which word means "not dependable or trusted"?
   - uncertain
   - ● unreliable
   - inconvenient
4. Which word is spelled correctly?
   - ● immediate
   - immeidate
   - immeidiate

Spelling Test

Ask someone to test you on the spelling words.

1. ____ 2. ____ 3. ____ 4. ____ 5. ____ 6. ____ 7. ____ 8. ____ 9. ____ 10. ____ 11. ____ 12. ____

5. Write the sentence correctly.

it's unconvenient for me to transpert that poretible torch imediately

It's inconvenient for me to transport that portable torch immediately.

82 ASSESSMENT 8 Spell & Write • EMC 4542 • ©2005 by Evan-Moor Corp.

Page 83

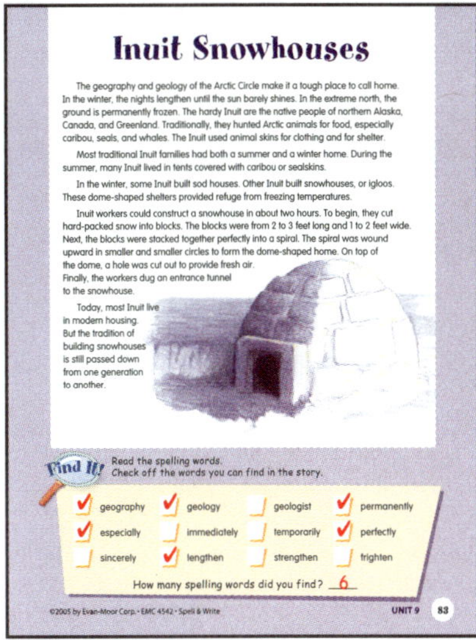

Inuit Snowhouses

The geography and geology of the Arctic Circle make it a tough place to call home. In the winter, the nights lengthen until the sun barely shines. In the extreme north, the ground is permanently frozen. The hardy Inuit are the native people of northern Alaska, Canada, and Greenland. Traditionally, they hunted Arctic animals for food, especially caribou, seals, and whales. The Inuit used animal skins for clothing and for shelter.

Most traditional Inuit families had both a summer and a winter home. During the summer, many Inuit lived in tents covered with caribou or sealskins.

In the winter, some Inuit built sod houses. Other Inuit built snowhouses, or igloos. These dome-shaped shelters provided refuge from freezing temperatures.

Inuit workers could construct a snowhouse in about two hours. To begin, they cut hard-packed snow into blocks. The blocks were from 2 to 3 feet long and 1 to 2 feet wide. Next, the blocks were stacked together perfectly into a spiral. The spiral was wound upward in smaller and smaller circles to form the dome-shaped home. On top of the dome, a hole was cut out to provide fresh air. Finally, the workers dug an entrance tunnel to the snowhouse.

Today, most Inuit live in modern housing. But the tradition of building snowhouses is still passed down from one generation to another.

Find It! Read the spelling words. Check off the words you can find in the story.

✔ geography	✔ geology	geologist	✔ permanently
✔ especially	immediately	temporarily	✔ perfectly
sincerely	✔ lengthen	strengthen	frighten

How many spelling words did you find? 6

©2005 by Evan-Moor Corp. • EMC 4542 • Spell & Write UNIT 9 83

Page 85

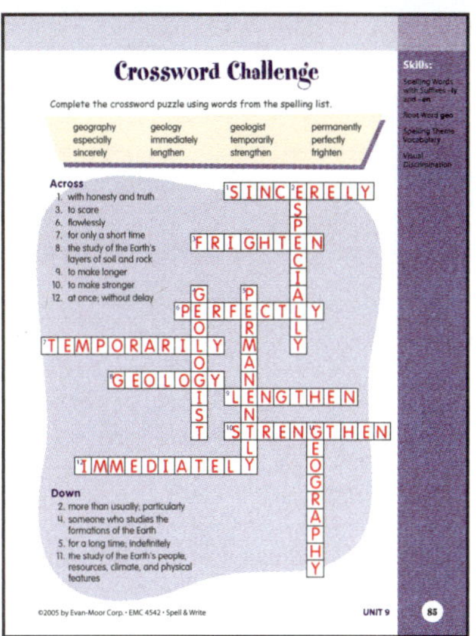

Crossword Challenge

Skills: Spelling Words with Suffixes -ly and -en; Root Word geo; Spelling Theme Vocabulary; Visual Discrimination

Complete the crossword puzzle using words from the spelling list.

geography, geology, geologist, permanently, especially, immediately, temporarily, perfectly, sincerely, lengthen, strengthen, frighten

Across
1. with honesty and truth — SINCERELY
3. to scare — FRIGHTEN
6. flawlessly — PERFECTLY
7. for only a short time — TEMPORARILY
8. the study of the Earth's layers of soil and rock — GEOLOGY
9. to make longer — LENGTHEN
10. to make stronger — STRENGTHEN
12. at once; without delay — IMMEDIATELY

Down
2. more than usually; particularly — ESPECIALLY
4. someone who studies the formations of the Earth — GEOLOGIST
5. for a long time; indefinitely — PERMANENTLY
11. the study of the Earth's people, resources, climate, and physical features — GEOGRAPHY

©2005 by Evan-Moor Corp. • EMC 4542 • Spell & Write UNIT 9 85

Page 86

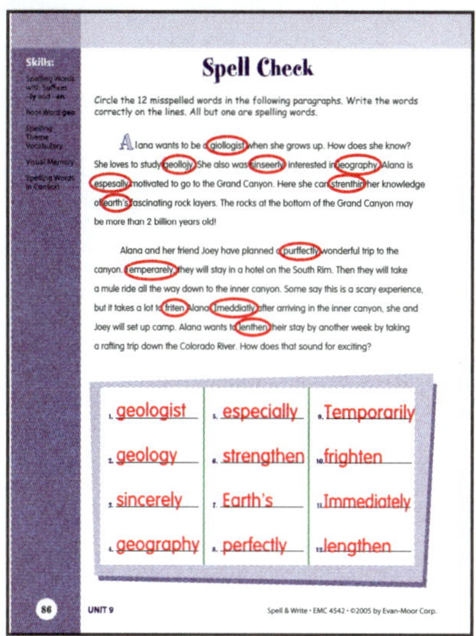

Spell Check

Skills: Spelling Words with Suffixes -ly and -en; Root Word geo; Spelling Theme Vocabulary; Visual Memory; Spelling Words in Context

Circle the 12 misspelled words in the following paragraphs. Write the words correctly on the lines. All but one are spelling words.

Alana wants to be a giollogist when she grows up. How does she know? She loves to study geollojy. She also was sinseerly interested in jeography. Alana is espesally motivated to go to the Grand Canyon. Here she can strenthin her knowledge of earth's fascinating rock layers. The rocks at the bottom of the Grand Canyon may be more than 2 billion years old!

Alana and her friend Joey have planned a purffectly wonderful trip to the canyon. Temperarely, they will stay in a hotel on the South Rim. Then they will take a mule ride all the way down to the inner canyon. Some say this is a scary experience, but it takes a lot to friten Alana. Imeddiatly after arriving in the inner canyon, she and Joey will set up camp. Alana wants to lenthen their stay by another week by taking a rafting trip down the Colorado River. How does that sound for exciting?

1. geologist	5. especially	9. Temporarily
2. geology	6. strengthen	10. frighten
3. sincerely	7. Earth's	11. Immediately
4. geography	8. perfectly	12. lengthen

86 UNIT 9 Spell & Write • EMC 4542 • ©2005 by Evan-Moor Corp.

Page 87

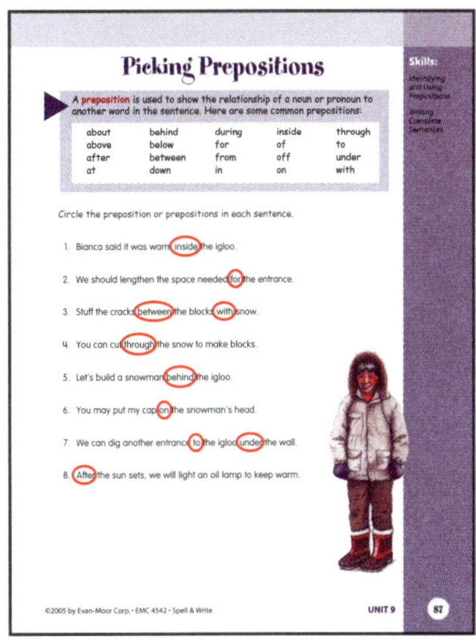

Picking Prepositions

Skills: Identifying and Using Prepositions; Writing Complete Sentences

A **preposition** is used to show the relationship of a noun or pronoun to another word in the sentence. Here are some common prepositions:

about	behind	during	inside	through
above	below	for	of	to
after	between	from	off	under
at	down	in	on	with

Circle the preposition or prepositions in each sentence.

1. Bianca said it was warm inside the igloo.
2. We should lengthen the space needed for the entrance.
3. Stuff the cracks between the blocks with snow.
4. You can cut through the snow to make blocks.
5. Let's build a snowman behind the igloo.
6. You may put my cap on the snowman's head.
7. We can dig another entrance to the igloo under the wall.
8. After the sun sets, we will light an oil lamp to keep warm.

©2005 by Evan-Moor Corp. • EMC 4542 • Spell & Write UNIT 9 87

Page 88

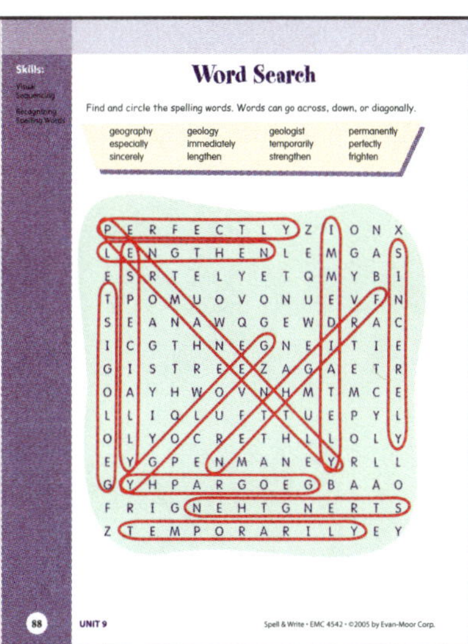

Word Search

Skills: Visual Sequencing; Recognizing Spelling Words

Find and circle the spelling words. Words can go across, down, or diagonally.

geography, geology, geologist, permanently, especially, immediately, temporarily, perfectly, sincerely, lengthen, strengthen, frighten

P	E	R	F	E	C	T	L	Y	Z	I	O	N	X
L	E	N	G	T	H	E	N	L	E	M	G	A	S
E	S	R	T	E	L	Y	E	T	Q	M	Y	B	I
T	P	O	M	U	O	V	O	N	U	E	V	F	N
S	E	A	N	A	W	Q	G	E	W	D	R	A	C
I	C	G	T	H	N	E	G	N	E	I	T	I	E
G	I	S	T	R	E	E	Z	A	G	A	E	T	R
O	A	Y	H	W	O	V	N	H	M	T	M	C	E
L	L	I	Q	L	U	F	T	T	U	E	P	Y	L
O	L	Y	O	C	R	E	T	H	L	L	O	L	Y
E	Y	G	P	E	N	M	A	N	E	Y	R	L	L
G	Y	H	P	A	R	G	O	E	G	B	A	A	O
F	R	I	G	N	E	H	T	G	N	E	R	T	S
Z	T	E	M	P	O	R	A	R	I	L	Y	E	Y

88 UNIT 9 Spell & Write • EMC 4542 • ©2005 by Evan-Moor Corp.

Page 90

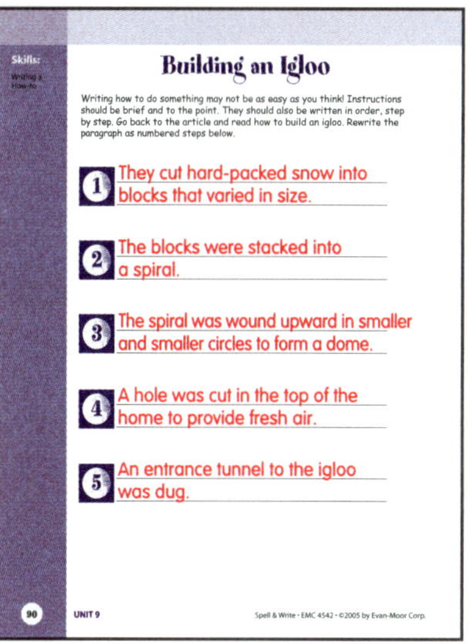

Building an Igloo

Skills: Writing a How-to

Writing how to do something may not be as easy as you think! Instructions should be brief and to the point. They should also be written in order, step by step. Go back to the article and read how to build an igloo. Rewrite the paragraph as numbered steps below.

1. They cut hard-packed snow into blocks that varied in size.
2. The blocks were stacked into a spiral.
3. The spiral was wound upward in smaller and smaller circles to form a dome.
4. A hole was cut in the top of the home to provide fresh air.
5. An entrance tunnel to the igloo was dug.

90 UNIT 9 Spell & Write • EMC 4542 • ©2005 by Evan-Moor Corp.

Page 91

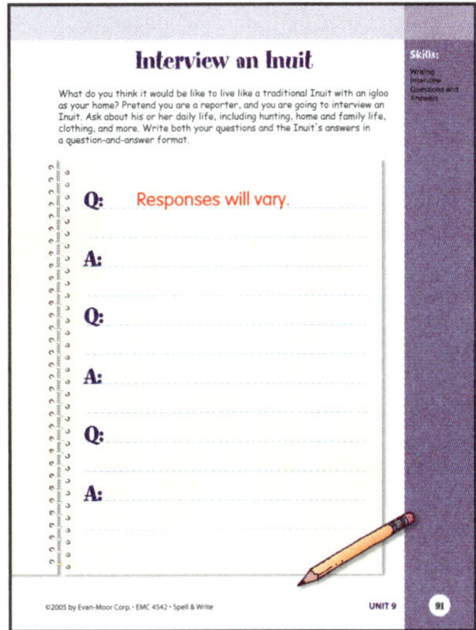

Interview an Inuit

Skills: Writing Interview Questions and Answers

What do you think it would be like to live like a traditional Inuit with an igloo as your home? Pretend you are a reporter, and you are going to interview an Inuit. Ask about his or her daily life, including hunting, home and family life, clothing, and more. Write both your questions and the Inuit's answers in a question-and-answer format.

Q: Responses will vary.

A:

Q:

A:

Q:

A:

©2005 by Evan-Moor Corp. • EMC 4542 • Spell & Write UNIT 9 91

Page 92

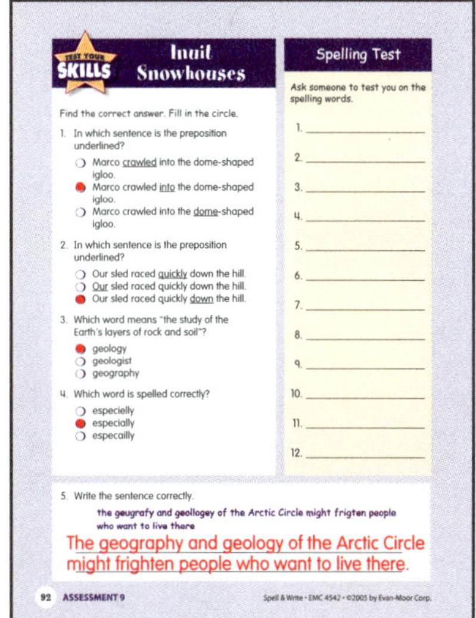

Test Your Skills: Inuit Snowhouses

Find the correct answer. Fill in the circle.

1. In which sentence is the preposition underlined?
   - ○ Marco crawled into the dome-shaped igloo. (crawled underlined)
   - ● Marco crawled into the dome-shaped igloo. (into underlined)
   - ○ Marco crawled into the dome-shaped igloo. (dome underlined)
2. In which sentence is the preposition underlined?
   - ○ Our sled raced quickly down the hill. (quickly underlined)
   - ○ Our sled raced quickly down the hill. (Our underlined)
   - ● Our sled raced quickly down the hill. (down underlined)
3. Which word means "the study of the Earth's layers of rock and soil"?
   - ● geology
   - ○ geologist
   - ○ geography
4. Which word is spelled correctly?
   - ○ especielly
   - ● especially
   - ○ especailly

Spelling Test

Ask someone to test you on the spelling words.

1. ____ 2. ____ 3. ____ 4. ____ 5. ____ 6. ____ 7. ____ 8. ____ 9. ____ 10. ____ 11. ____ 12. ____

5. Write the sentence correctly.

the geugrafy and geollogey of the Arctic Circle might frigten people who want to live there

The geography and geology of the Arctic Circle might frighten people who want to live there.

92 ASSESSMENT 9 Spell & Write • EMC 4542 • ©2005 by Evan-Moor Corp.

Page 93

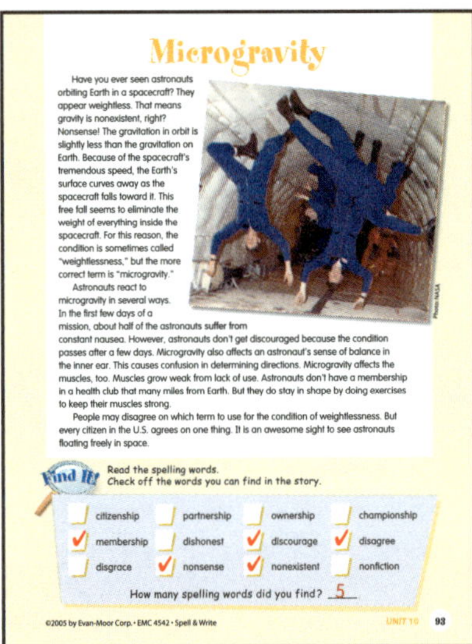

Page 95

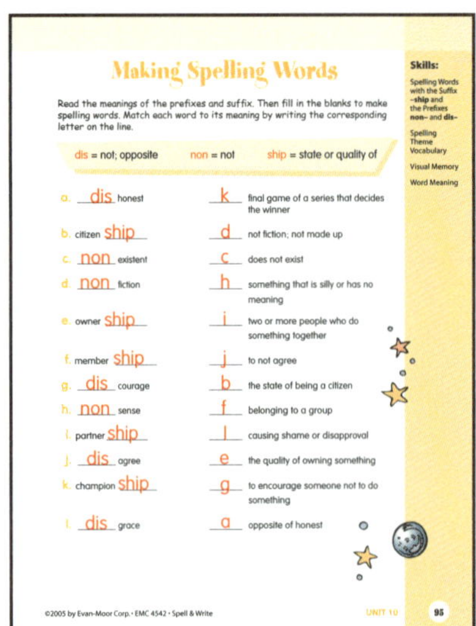

Page 96

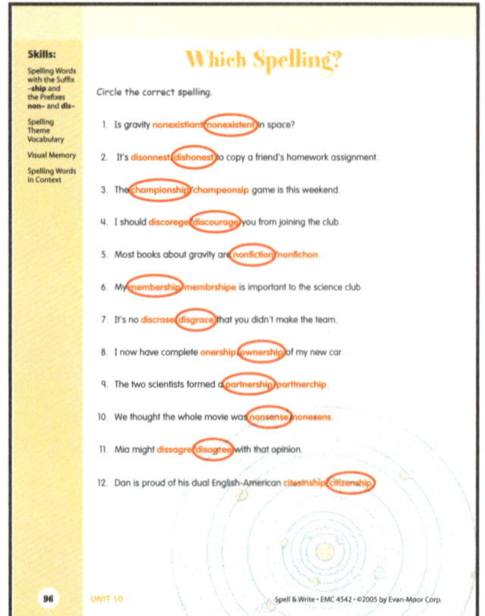

Page 97

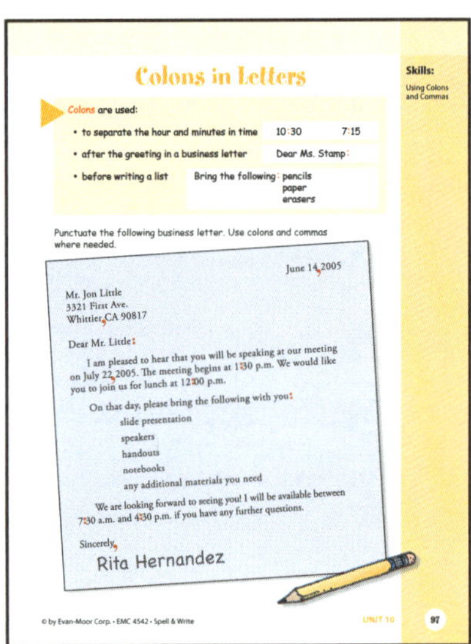

Page 98

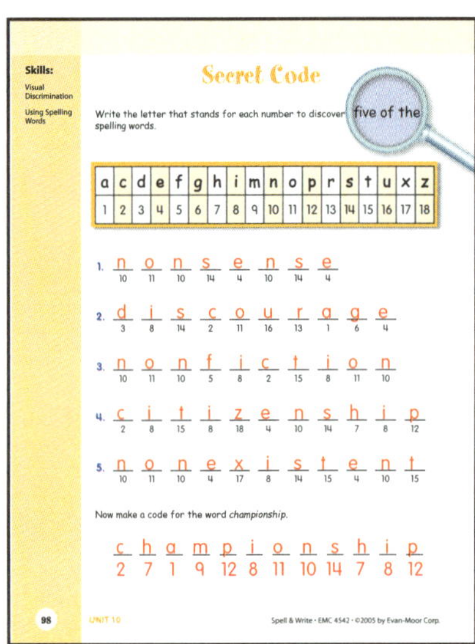

Page 100

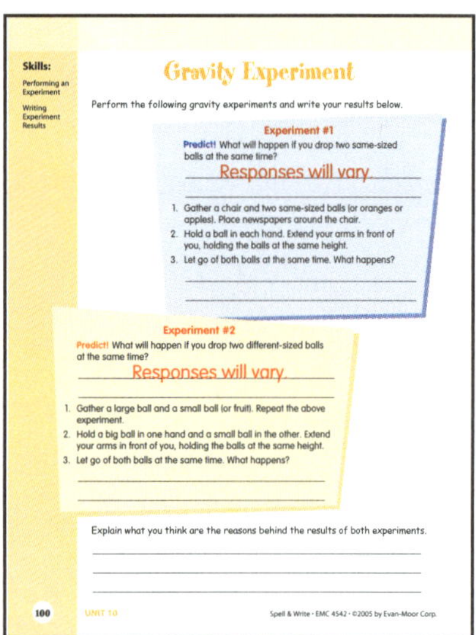

Page 101

Page 102

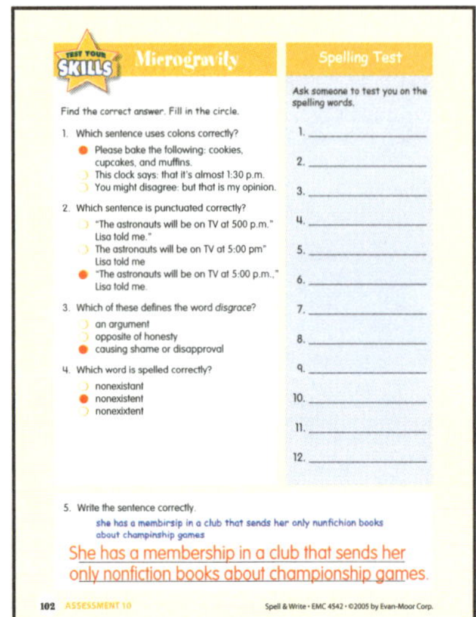

Page 103

Meat-Eating Plants

When you think of a predator, you probably don't picture a plant. You may want to rethink this! Most green plants make their own food. Carnivorous plants do, too, but they also need a reliable source of meat on the menu. These plants often grow in swampy soil where nitrogen and other nutrients are sparse. They get what they need by trapping and digesting insects and other small animals that have the misfortune of getting too close.

The Venus' flytrap grows in North and South Carolina. This deadly plant can attract a fly to its sweet nectar. Its hinged leaves, covered with tiny hairs and lined with bristles, are genuine traps. When the fly brushes against several hairs, the leaves snap closed. The bristles trap the fly inside, and the prey is digested within 10 days.

The pitcher plant of Southeast Asia is about three feet tall. Water and digestive juices collect inside its slippery "pitcher." Attracted to the abundant, sweet-smelling nectar, insects, frogs, and small rodents slide in and do not reappear.

Sundews are found around the world. The leaves are lined with miniature hairs tipped with sticky, sweet droplets. If an inquisitive insect gets trapped in a droplet, the leaf curls around the victim and digests it within five days.

Find It! Read the spelling words. Check off the words you can find in the story.

- [x] reappear
- [x] rethink
- [ ] misspell
- [x] misfortune
- [ ] misdirect
- [ ] zealous
- [x] miniature
- [x] inquisitive
- [x] genuine
- [x] reliable
- [x] sparse
- [x] abundant

How many spelling words did you find? 9

©2005 by Evan-Moor Corp. • EMC 4542 • Spell & Write UNIT 11 103

Page 105

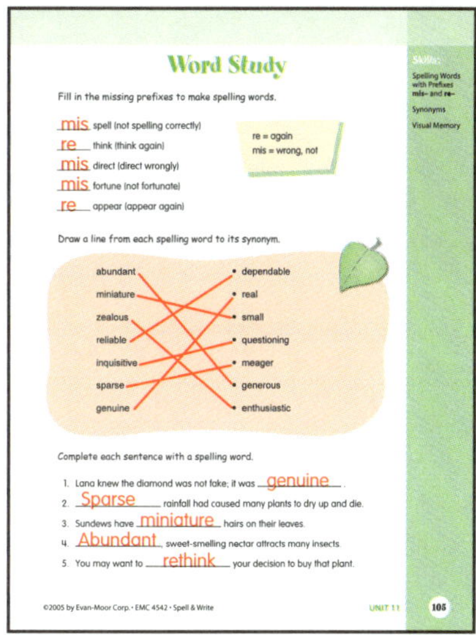

Word Study

Skills: Spelling Words with Prefixes mis- and re-; Synonyms; Visual Memory

Fill in the missing prefixes to make spelling words.

mis spell (not spelling correctly)
re think (think again)
mis direct (direct wrongly)
mis fortune (not fortunate)
re appear (appear again)

re = again
mis = wrong, not

Draw a line from each spelling word to its synonym.

abundant	dependable
miniature	real
zealous	small
reliable	questioning
inquisitive	meager
sparse	generous
genuine	enthusiastic

Complete each sentence with a spelling word.

1. Lana knew the diamond was not fake; it was genuine.
2. Sparse rainfall had caused many plants to dry up and die.
3. Sundews have miniature hairs on their leaves.
4. Abundant sweet-smelling nectar attracts many insects.
5. You may want to rethink your decision to buy that plant.

©2005 by Evan-Moor Corp. • EMC 4542 • Spell & Write UNIT 11 105

Page 106

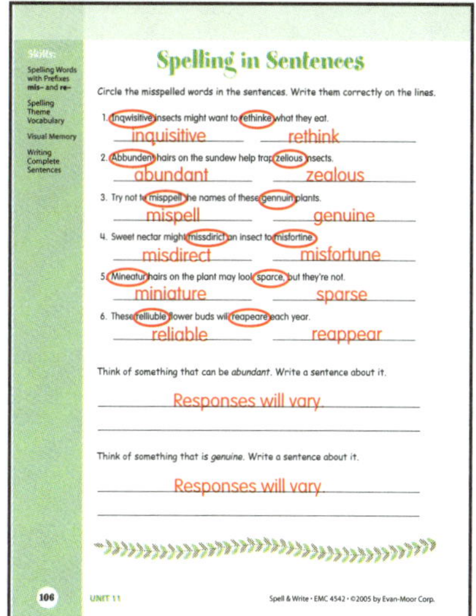

Spelling in Sentences

Skills: Spelling Words with Prefixes mis- and re-; Spelling Theme Vocabulary; Visual Memory; Writing Complete Sentences

Circle the misspelled words in the sentences. Write them correctly on the lines.

1. Inqwisitive insects might want to rethinke what they eat.
   inquisitive rethink
2. Abbundent hairs on the sundew help trap zelious insects.
   abundant zealous
3. Try not to misppell the names of these gennuin plants.
   mispell genuine
4. Sweet nectar might missdirct an insect to misfortine.
   misdirect misfortune
5. Mineatur hairs on the plant may look sparce, but they're not.
   miniature sparse
6. These relliable flower buds will reapeare each year.
   reliable reappear

Think of something that can be abundant. Write a sentence about it.

Responses will vary.

Think of something that is genuine. Write a sentence about it.

Responses will vary.

106 UNIT 11 Spell & Write • EMC 4542 • ©2005 by Evan-Moor Corp.

Page 107

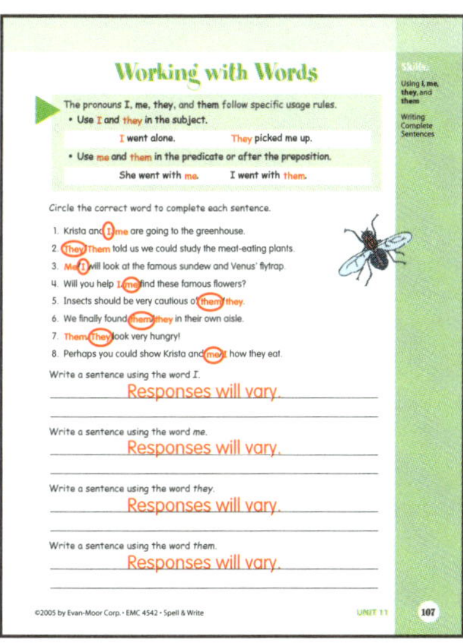

Working with Words

Skills: Using I, me, they, and them; Writing Complete Sentences

The pronouns **I**, **me**, **they**, and **them** follow specific usage rules.

- Use I and they in the subject.

  I went alone. They picked me up.

- Use me and them in the predicate or after the preposition.

  She went with me. I went with them.

Circle the correct word to complete each sentence.

1. Krista and (I) / me are going to the greenhouse.
2. (They) / Them told us we could study the meat-eating plants.
3. Me / (I) will look at the famous sundew and Venus' flytrap.
4. Will you help I / (me) find these famous flowers?
5. Insects should be very cautious of (them) / they.
6. We finally found (them) / they in their own aisle.
7. Them / (They) look very hungry!
8. Perhaps you could show Krista and (me) / I how they eat.

Write a sentence using the word *I*.

Responses will vary.

Write a sentence using the word *me*.

Responses will vary.

Write a sentence using the word *they*.

Responses will vary.

Write a sentence using the word *them*.

Responses will vary.

©2005 by Evan-Moor Corp. • EMC 4542 • Spell & Write UNIT 11 107

Page 108

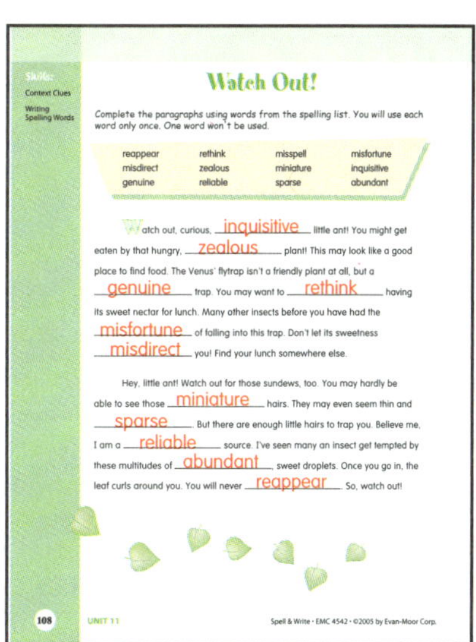

Watch Out!

Skills: Context Clues; Writing Spelling Words

Complete the paragraphs using words from the spelling list. You will use each word only once. One word won't be used.

reappear	rethink	misspell	misfortune
misdirect	zealous	miniature	inquisitive
genuine	reliable	sparse	abundant

Watch out, curious, inquisitive little ant! You might get eaten by that hungry, zealous plant! This may look like a good place to find food. The Venus' flytrap isn't a friendly plant at all, but a genuine trap. You may want to rethink having its sweet nectar for lunch. Many other insects before you have had the misfortune of falling into this trap. Don't let its sweetness misdirect you! Find your lunch somewhere else.

Hey, little ant! Watch out for those sundews, too. You may hardly be able to see those miniature hairs. They may even seem thin and sparse. But there are enough little hairs to trap you. Believe me, I am a reliable source. I've seen many an insect get tempted by these multitudes of abundant, sweet droplets. Once you go in, the leaf curls around you. You will never reappear. So, watch out!

108 UNIT 11 Spell & Write • EMC 4542 • ©2005 by Evan-Moor Corp.

Page 110

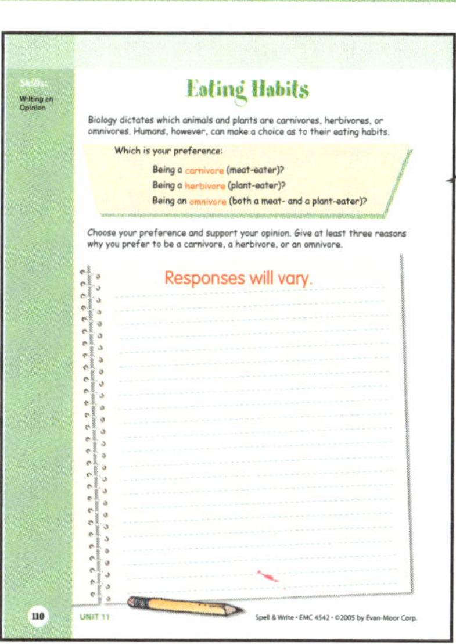

Eating Habits

Skills: Writing an Opinion

Biology dictates which animals and plants are carnivores, herbivores, or omnivores. Humans, however, can make a choice as to their eating habits.

Which is your preference:

Being a carnivore (meat-eater)?
Being a herbivore (plant-eater)?
Being an omnivore (both a meat- and a plant-eater)?

Choose your preference and support your opinion. Give at least three reasons why you prefer to be a carnivore, a herbivore, or an omnivore.

Responses will vary.

110 UNIT 11 Spell & Write • EMC 4542 • ©2005 by Evan-Moor Corp.

Page 111

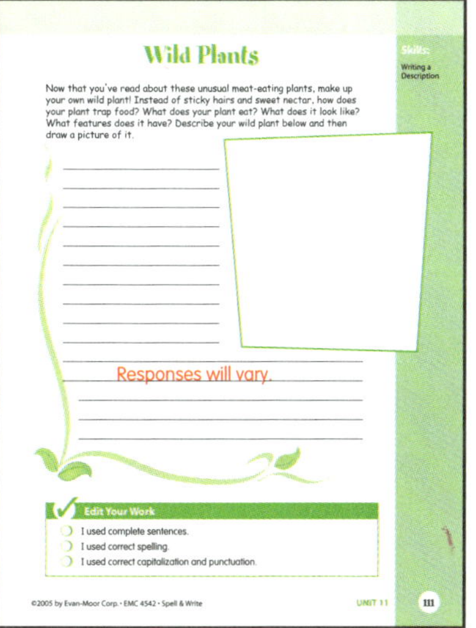

Wild Plants

Skills: Writing a Description

Now that you've read about these unusual meat-eating plants, make up your own wild plant! Instead of sticky hairs and sweet nectar, how does your plant trap food? What does your plant eat? What does it look like? What features does it have? Describe your wild plant below and then draw a picture of it.

Responses will vary.

Edit Your Work

- I used complete sentences.
- I used correct spelling.
- I used correct capitalization and punctuation.

©2005 by Evan-Moor Corp. • EMC 4542 • Spell & Write UNIT 11 111

Page 112

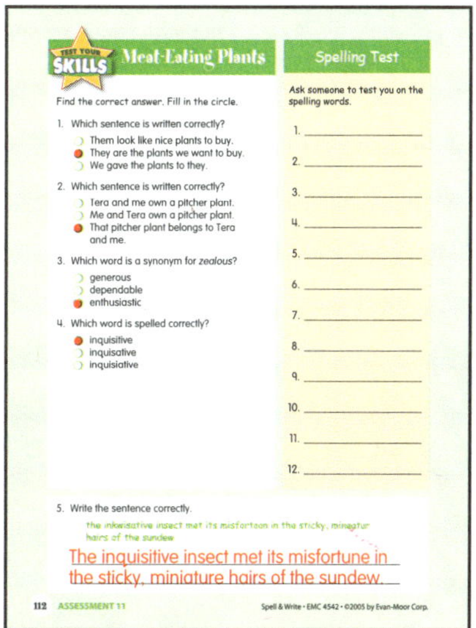

Test Your Skills: Meat-Eating Plants

Find the correct answer. Fill in the circle.

1. Which sentence is written correctly?
   - ○ Them look like nice plants to buy.
   - ● They are the plants we want to buy.
   - ○ We gave the plants to they.
2. Which sentence is written correctly?
   - ○ Tera and me own a pitcher plant.
   - ○ Me and Tera own a pitcher plant.
   - ● That pitcher plant belongs to Tera and me.
3. Which word is a synonym for *zealous*?
   - ○ generous
   - ○ dependable
   - ● enthusiastic
4. Which word is spelled correctly?
   - ● inquisitive
   - ○ inquisative
   - ○ inquisiative

Spelling Test

Ask someone to test you on the spelling words.

1. ____
2. ____
3. ____
4. ____
5. ____
6. ____
7. ____
8. ____
9. ____
10. ____
11. ____
12. ____

5. Write the sentence correctly.

the inkwisative insect met its misfortoon in the sticky, minigtur hairs of the sundew

The inquisitive insect met its misfortune in the sticky, miniature hairs of the sundew.

112 ASSESSMENT 11 Spell & Write • EMC 4542 • ©2005 by Evan-Moor Corp.

Page 113

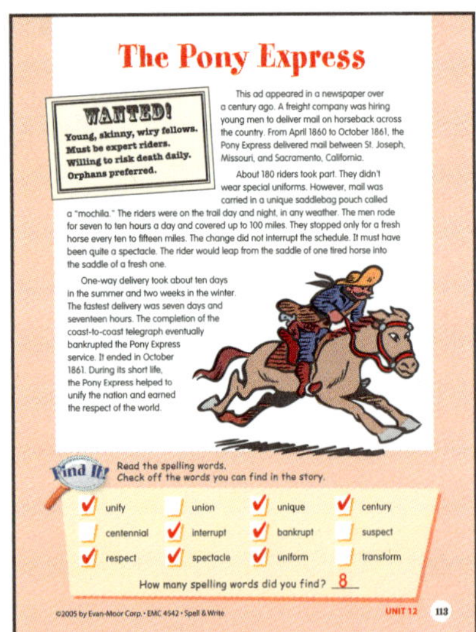

The Pony Express

WANTED!
Young, skinny, wiry fellows.
Must be expert riders.
Willing to risk death daily.
Orphans preferred.

This ad appeared in a newspaper over a century ago. A freight company was hiring young men to deliver mail on horseback across the country. From April 1860 to October 1861, the Pony Express delivered mail between St. Joseph, Missouri, and Sacramento, California.

About 180 riders took part. They didn't wear special uniforms. However, mail was carried in a unique saddlebag pouch called a "mochila." The riders were on the trail day and night, in any weather. The men rode for seven to ten hours a day and covered up to 100 miles. They stopped only for a fresh horse every ten to fifteen miles. The change did not interrupt the schedule. It must have been quite a spectacle. The rider would leap from the saddle of one tired horse into the saddle of a fresh one.

One-way delivery took about ten days in the summer and two weeks in the winter. The fastest delivery was seven days and seventeen hours. The completion of the coast-to-coast telegraph eventually bankrupted the Pony Express service. It ended in October 1861. During its short life, the Pony Express helped to unify the nation and earned the respect of the world.

Find It! Read the spelling words. Check off the words you can find in the story.

✔ unify	union	✔ unique	✔ century
centennial	✔ interrupt	✔ bankrupt	suspect
✔ respect	✔ spectacle	✔ uniform	transform

How many spelling words did you find? 8

©2005 by Evan-Moor Corp. • EMC 4542 • Spell & Write UNIT 12 113

Page 115

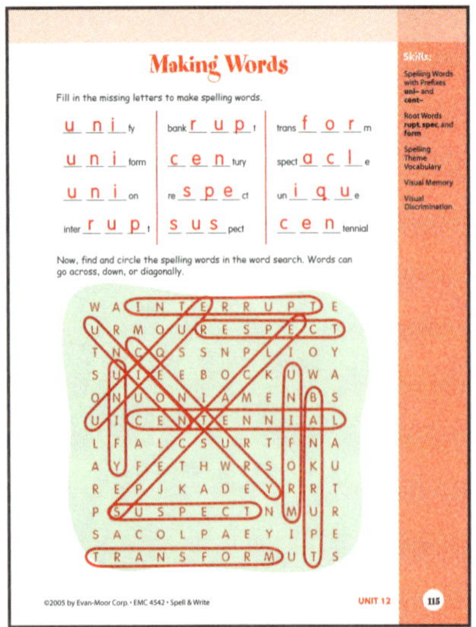

Making Words

Fill in the missing letters to make spelling words.

u n i fy	bank r u p t	trans f o r m
u n i form	c e n tury	spect a c l e
u n i on	re s p e ct	un i q u e
inter r u p t	s u s pect	c e n tennial

Now, find and circle the spelling words in the word search. Words can go across, down, or diagonally.

```
W A I N T E R R U P T E
U R M O U R E S P E C T
T N C S S N P L I O Y
S U E E B O C K U W A
O N U O N I A M E N B S
U I C E N T E N N I A L
L F A L C S U R T F N A
A Y F E T H W R S O K U
R E P J K A D E Y R R T
P S U S P E C T N M U R
S A C O L P A E Y I P E
T R A N S F O R M U T S
```

©2005 by Evan-Moor Corp. • EMC 4542 • Spell & Write UNIT 12 115

Page 116

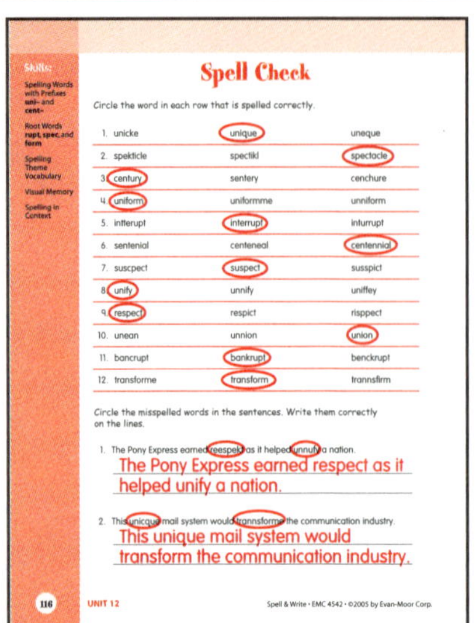

Spell Check

Circle the word in each row that is spelled correctly.

1.	unicke	(unique)	uneque
2.	spektacle	spectikl	(spectacle)
3.	(century)	sentery	cenchure
4.	(uniform)	uniformme	unniform
5.	interupt	(interrupt)	inturrupt
6.	sentenial	centeneal	(centennial)
7.	suscpect	(suspect)	susspict
8.	(unify)	unnify	unifey
9.	(respect)	respict	rispect
10.	unean	unnion	(union)
11.	bancrupt	(bankrupt)	benckrupt
12.	transforme	(transform)	trannsfirm

Circle the misspelled words in the sentences. Write them correctly on the lines.

1. The Pony Express earned reespekt as it helped unnufy a nation.
The Pony Express earned respect as it helped unify a nation.

2. This unicque mail system would transforme the communication industry.
This unique mail system would transform the communication industry.

116 UNIT 12 Spell & Write • EMC 4542 • ©2005 by Evan-Moor Corp.

Page 117

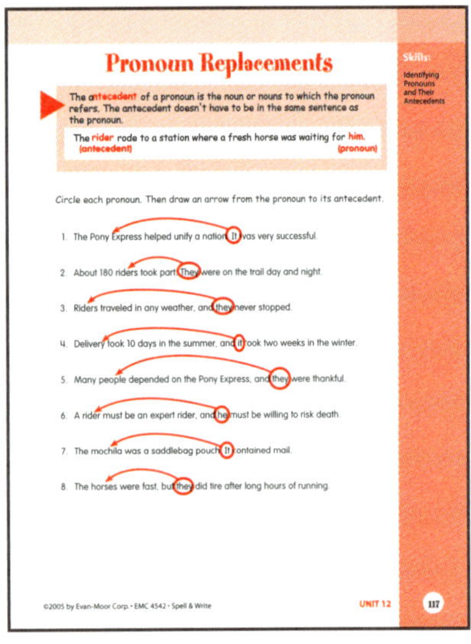

Pronoun Replacements

The antecedent of a pronoun is the noun or nouns to which the pronoun refers. The antecedent doesn't have to be in the same sentence as the pronoun.

The rider rode to a station where a fresh horse was waiting for him.
(antecedent) (pronoun)

Circle each pronoun. Then draw an arrow from the pronoun to its antecedent.

1. The Pony Express helped unify a nation. (It) was very successful.
2. About 180 riders took part. (They) were on the trail day and night.
3. Riders traveled in any weather, and (they) never stopped.
4. Delivery took 10 days in the summer, and (it) took two weeks in the winter.
5. Many people depended on the Pony Express, and (they) were thankful.
6. A rider must be an expert rider, and (he) must be willing to risk death.
7. The mochila was a saddlebag pouch. (It) contained mail.
8. The horses were fast, but (they) did tire after long hours of running.

©2005 by Evan-Moor Corp. • EMC 4542 • Spell & Write UNIT 12 117

Page 118

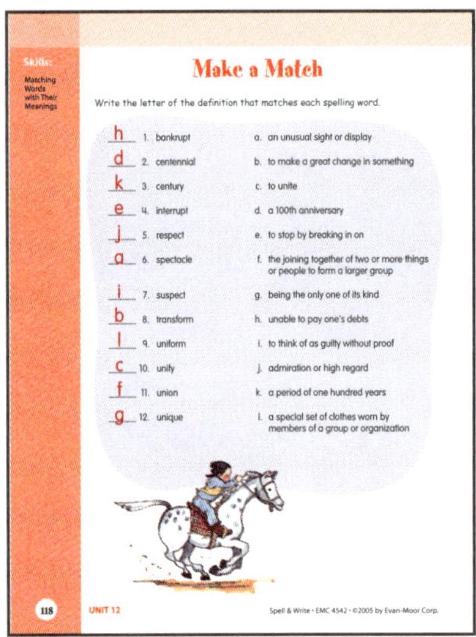

Make a Match

Write the letter of the definition that matches each spelling word.

h	1. bankrupt	a. an unusual sight or display
d	2. centennial	b. to make a great change in something
k	3. century	c. to unite
e	4. interrupt	d. a 100th anniversary
j	5. respect	e. to stop by breaking in on
a	6. spectacle	f. the joining together of two or more things or people to form a larger group
i	7. suspect	g. being the only one of its kind
b	8. transform	h. unable to pay one's debts
l	9. uniform	i. to think of as guilty without proof
c	10. unify	j. admiration or high regard
f	11. union	k. a period of one hundred years
g	12. unique	l. a special set of clothes worn by members of a group or organization

118 UNIT 12 Spell & Write • EMC 4542 • ©2005 by Evan-Moor Corp.

Page 120

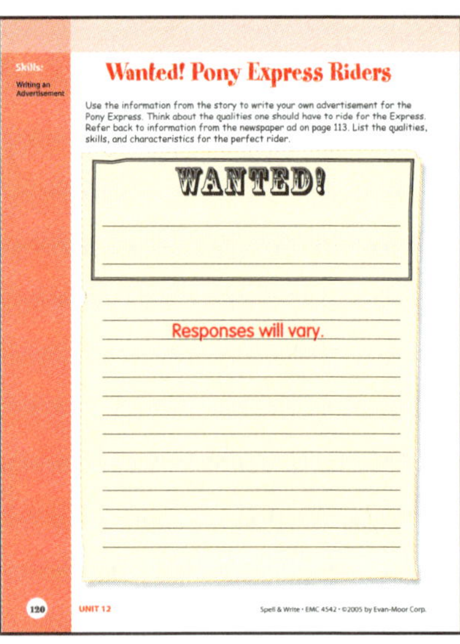

Wanted! Pony Express Riders

Use the information from the story to write your own advertisement for the Pony Express. Think about the qualities one should have to ride for the Express. Refer back to information from the newspaper ad on page 113. List the qualities, skills, and characteristics for the perfect rider.

WANTED!

Responses will vary.

120 UNIT 12 Spell & Write • EMC 4542 • ©2005 by Evan-Moor Corp.

Page 121

On the Trail

You are a Pony Express rider. Write about a day in your life on the trail. Where are you going? What kind of mail are you carrying? Who do you meet along the way? What kind of difficulties do you face? Write about it below.

Responses will vary.

Edit Your Work
- I used complete sentences.
- I used correct spelling.
- I used correct capitalization and punctuation.

©2005 by Evan-Moor Corp. • EMC 4542 • Spell & Write UNIT 12 121

Page 122

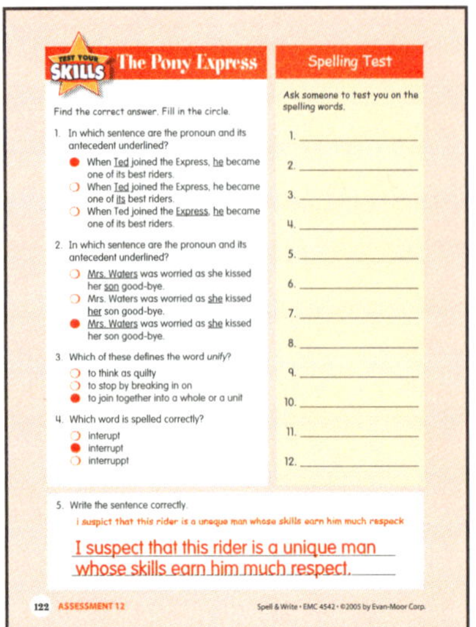

Test Your Skills: The Pony Express

Find the correct answer. Fill in the circle.

1. In which sentence are the pronoun and its antecedent underlined?
   - ● When Ted joined the Express, he became one of its best riders.
   - ○ When Ted joined the Express, he became one of its best riders.
   - ○ When Ted joined the Express, he became one of its best riders.
2. In which sentence are the pronoun and its antecedent underlined?
   - ○ Mrs. Waters was worried as she kissed her son good-bye.
   - ○ Mrs. Waters was worried as she kissed her son good-bye.
   - ● Mrs. Waters was worried as she kissed her son good-bye.
3. Which of these defines the word unify?
   - ○ to think as guilty
   - ○ to stop by breaking in on
   - ● to join together into a whole or a unit
4. Which word is spelled correctly?
   - ○ interupt
   - ● interrupt
   - ○ interrupt

Spelling Test

Ask someone to test you on the spelling words.

1. 2. 3. 4. 5. 6. 7. 8. 9. 10. 11. 12.

5. Write the sentence correctly.
I suspect that this rider is a uneque man whose skills earn him much respeck.
I suspect that this rider is a unique man whose skills earn him much respect.

122 ASSESSMENT 12 Spell & Write • EMC 4542 • ©2005 by Evan-Moor Corp.